The Poster Book of DINOSAURS
Dr David Norman

INTRODUCTION — 3

SAURISCHIA

'COELUROSAURS'	6
ORNITHOMIMOSAURS AND OVIRAPTOROSAURS	8
DROMAEOSAURIDS	10
'CARNOSAURS'	12
TYRANNOSAURIDS	14
PROSAUROPODS	16
DIPLODOCIDS	18
CAMARASAURIDS AND BRACHIOSAURIDS	20
MISCELLANEOUS SAUROPODS	22

ORNITHISCHIA

FABROSAURIDS AND HETERODONTOSAURIDS	24
HYPSILOPHODONTIDS	26
IGUANODONTIDS	28
HADROSAURIDS I	30
HADROSAURIDS II	32
PSITTACOSAURS AND PROTOCERATOPIDS	34
CERATOPIDS I	36
CERATOPIDS II	38
PACHYCEPHALOSAURS	40
STEGOSAURIDS	42
NODOSAURIDS	44
ANKYLOSAURIDS	46

GLOSSARY AND INDEX — 48

HODDER AND STOUGHTON
LONDON   SYDNEY   AUCKLAND   TORONTO

British Library Cataloguing in Publication Data

Norman, David, 1930-
The poster book of dinosaurs.
1. Dinosaurs — For children
I. Title
567.9'1

ISBN 0-340-48639-2

Text and illustrations copyright © Salamander Books Ltd. 1987

First published in Great Britain 1988 in association with
Salamander Books Ltd., 52 Bedford Row, London WC1R 4LR

Published by Hodder and Stoughton Children's Books,
a division of Hodder and Stoughton Ltd,
Mill Road, Dunton Green, Sevenoaks, Kent TN13 2YJ.

Colour dinosaur artwork by John Sibbick
Skeletal drawings by Denise Blagden and David Nicholls

Printed in Belgium by Henri Proost et Cie, Turnhout

All rights reserved

INTRODUCTION

This is a picture book all about dinosaurs. It is arranged so that you can see at a glance, on each spread of the book, beautiful colour pictures of nearly all of the major groups of dinosaurs that are known today. These pictures can be pulled out and used as posters, as presents for friends or left in place if you want to keep the book together. In addition to the colour pictures, there are also pages of technical drawings of dinosaurs and lots of facts that will help you to understand how we know what we do about these animals.

When were dinosaurs first discovered?

Dinosaurs were discovered quite late in the history of the study of fossils. To be precise, they were first named by a famous British scientist called Professor Richard Owen, at a meeting of the British Association for the Advancement of Science in 1841. Fossils, including no doubt many dinosaur remains, had been known for centuries before that time, but dinosaurs were simply not seen as anything new or interesting until Professor Owen's announcement.

Professor Owen made his discovery after being asked to study all the fossil reptiles that had been found in Britain up to that time. Having looked carefully at some of these fossils, especially *Iguanodon* (pages 28-29) and *Hylaeosaurus* (pages 44-45) which had been discovered in the 1820s and 1830s, he realised that although they had been thought to be giant fossil lizards, they really did not look at all like lizards do today. In fact, as he very rightly pointed out, they bore more of a resemblance to elephants! Their great big legs were tucked under the body to support its tremendous weight, whereas all living reptiles, be they lizards, tortoises or crocodiles, crawl along the ground with their legs sticking out from the sides of their bodies.

Sedimentation (below)
Weathering is responsible for the formation of sedimentary rocks. Wind, water, rain, and ice action erode exposed rock; the silt is carried down streams and rivers to lakes, lagoons or deltas where it may be deposited in layers. Land-living animals, such as dinosaurs are most likely to be buried and fossilised in such areas. In order for fossils to be discovered, the layers of sediment have to be lifted by earth movements so that erosion can start again.

The Geological Timescale (right)
On the right is an attempt to give some idea of just how old the Earth is. The Earth began to take shape sometime between 4,500 and 5,000 million years ago; it started off as a cloud of dust and gas. At first, the surface would have been incredibly hot, but as it began to cool down the steam turned to water and formed the oceans and more normal weather conditions appeared. After the first 2,000 million years, the first living things (small slimy green algae) appear in pools of water. Plants of one sort or another are all that lived on Earth for the next 2,500 million years. Then the animals appear, first as simple worms and snails, then as fish, amphibians, reptiles and finally the mammals and birds. The dinosaurs that interest us first appeared 200 million years ago and lived during the Triassic, Jurassic and Cretaceous Periods.

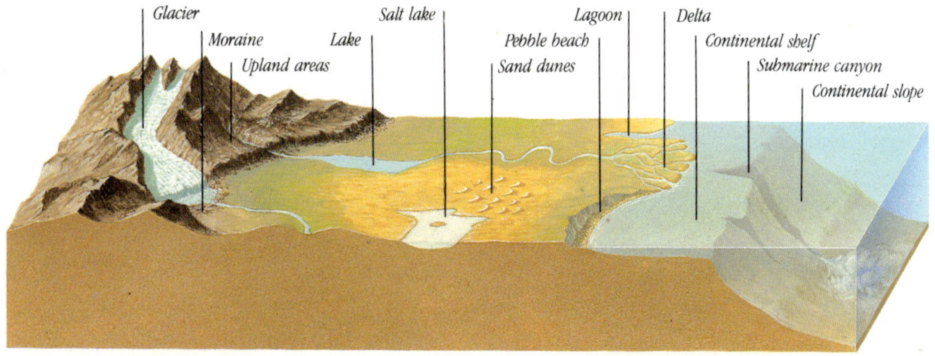

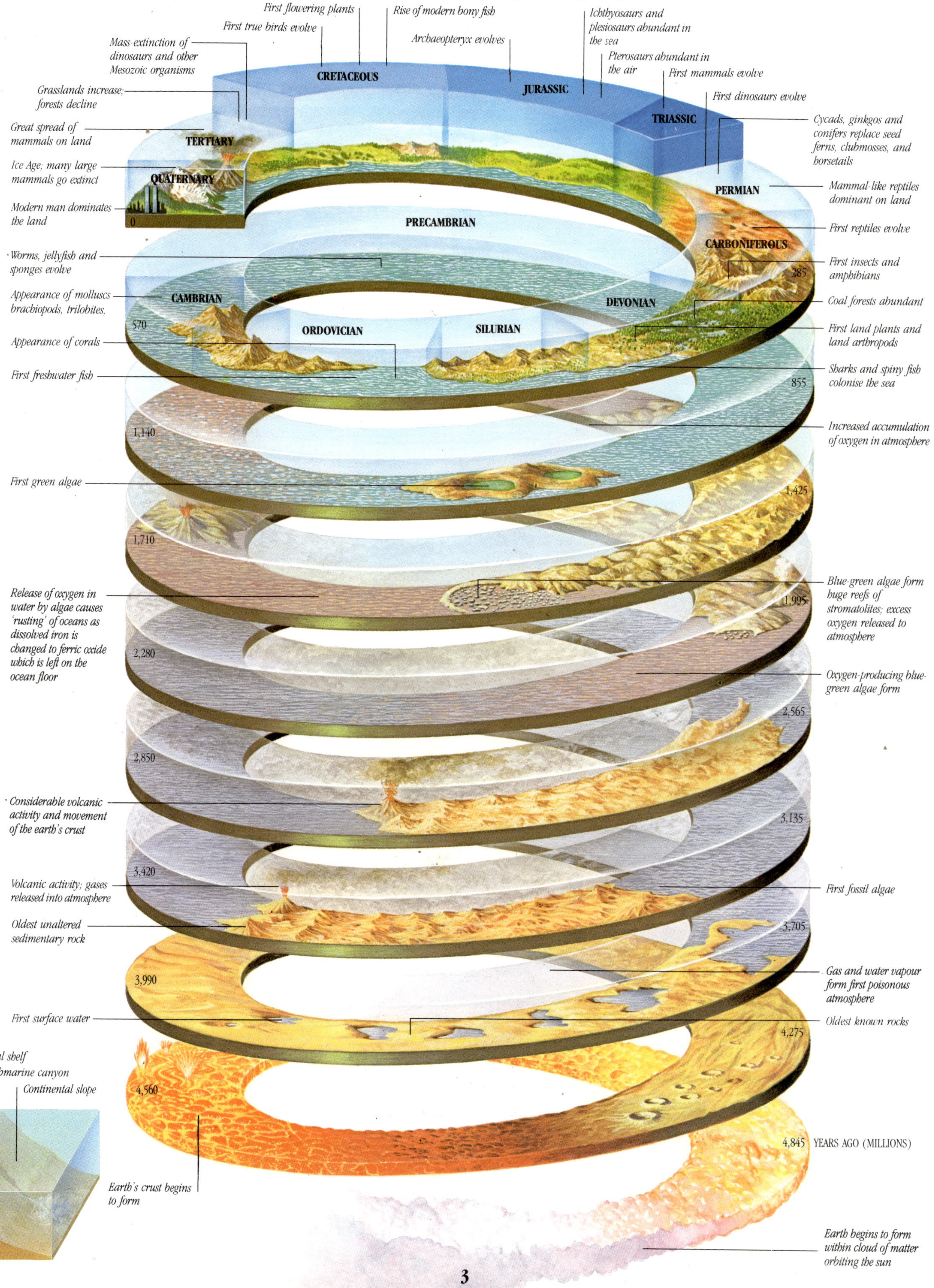

To recognise the fact that these fossil animals were huge and probably quite terrifying creatures he gave them the name Dinosaur, which comes from the Greek, the ancient scientific language often used for naming animals and plants; 'Deinos' meaning 'terrifying' or 'fearfully great' and 'Sauros' meaning 'reptile' or 'crawling animal'. The idea of gigantic 'terrible reptiles' seems to have caught everybody's imagination because as soon as Owen had named them everyone started looking for dinosaurs—and finding them—in rocks in various parts of the world.

What were dinosaurs?

Dinosaurs are not, therefore, just any old sort of prehistoric animal. To start with they have to be reptiles, which means that fossil fish, amphibians, mammals and birds are not dinosaurs—although we shall come back to birds later in this Introduction. Giant fossil animals such as woolly mammoths and sabre-tooth tigers are definitely not dinosaurs. Also, within the group of animals known as reptiles there are lots of types that are not dinosaurs because they did not walk with their legs tucked underneath the body as dinosaurs did. The giant prehistoric sea reptiles such as the plesiosaurs and ichthyosaurs are not dinosaurs; nor are the giant prehistoric flying reptiles, the pterodactyls. These groups are often mistakenly called dinosaurs because, not only are they large, they lived at about the same time as dinosaurs, which takes us on to the next question.

When did dinosaurs live?

On the Geological Timescale illustration shown here the time when dinosaurs lived on Earth has been picked out of the top spiral. It covers the best part of three geological

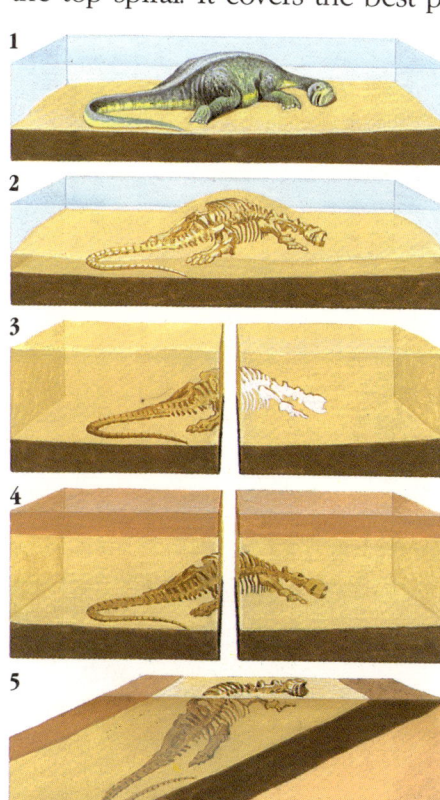

Fossilisation (left)
An essential requirement for the formation of a fossil is that after the organism dies (**1**) and the soft tissue rots away leaving (in this example) the bony skeleton, it should be rapidly buried by sediment (**2**). This normally occurs in rivers, lakes, or the sea into which the carcasses of land-living animals may be washed. Two processes may then occur (**3**). The organic material in the bones decays and may be replaced by minerals from water seeping through the sedimentary rocks: permineralisation (**left**). The bony structure may even be replaced entirely by minerals: petrification. Alternatively the bones may dissolve leaving a hollow mould (**right**) which may be filled later by minerals which form a solid replica of the bone: a natural cast (**4 right**). Land movements and erosion may then lead to exposure of the fossil (**5**).

periods; the Triassic, Jurassic and Cretaceous Periods, amounting to about 140 million years – a staggeringly long time. To put that into some sort of perspective, the species of Mankind, to which we belong, has only been on Earth for about 100,000 years. It is worth noting that Prehistoric Men did not live, and fight, with dinosaurs. Dinosaurs became extinct about 64 million years ago and the first Prehistoric Men did not appear until 2 million years ago.

Why did dinosaurs become extinct?

Precisely why dinosaurs became extinct is something that has been argued about for many years now. The number of different theories that have been suggested is enormous; someone has counted as many as 95 different ideas! They range from the plain potty ones, such as the suggestion that Martians came down to Earth and blasted them all to death with ray guns, to the idea that they all died of either constipation or diarrhoea brought on by a change in the plants that were living at the time. It is now accepted by most experts that there are really only two main types of theory to discuss.

Firstly, there is the cosmic theory, which argues that something from outer space must have affected life on Earth 64 million years ago. The most popular candidate for this sudden change is a large meteorite. A huge meteor crashing into the Earth could have caused immense damage, throwing enormous amounts of dust and steam into the air and cutting out the Sun for months or even

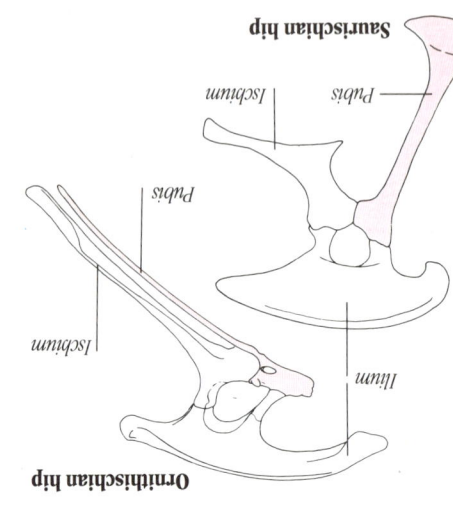

Dinosaur hips (left and below)

In this book the dinosaurs are split into two groups – ornithischian and saurischian. Ornithischian means 'bird-hipped' because the hip bones are arranged just as they are in living birds (see how the bone called the pubis lies next to the ischium). Saurischians, 'reptile hipped', dinosaurs have their hip bones arranged as in reptiles. *Stegosaurus* (below left) is a typical ornithischian while *Tyrannosaurus* (below right) is a typical saurischian.

years. The effect of all this would be to make the Earth very dark and cold which would have killed off all sorts of animals and plants, including the dinosaurs.

The second theory is related to the knowledge that the continents of the Earth have moved around. This is a process known as Continental Drift and occurs because the continents sit on the thin skin of the Earth which is known as the crust. Inside the crust, the rocks of the Earth are hot and liquid, like the lava that comes from volcanoes. As the hot liquid rock moves around inside the Earth it pulls the crust, which in turn moves the continents, as though they were on a giant conveyor belt.

During much of the time when dinosaurs lived, the world was a very warm place, ideal for giant reptiles. Towards the end of the reign of the dinosaurs we can see that the plants become gradually more cold-loving types, which suggests that the weather patterns of the world were slowly changing to ones that the dinosaurs would not have liked. We also begin to find more and more of the animals that are very good at living in colder conditions, such as mammals with furry rather than scaly skins. The explanation for this is that the continents had moved so much during the 140 million years dinosaurs were around that new weather conditions were created on a world-wide scale; this change hastened the end of dinosaurs and other warmth loving creatures.

The first of these theories suggests that the changes took place very suddenly following the impact of a meteorite, while the other seems to support a slower and altogether more gradual change as the weather deteriorated over many thousands or even millions of years. At the moment there is no way of knowing which of these theories is correct. On the one hand, the scientists who believe in the meteorite theory claim that they can prove that the dinosaurs died out very suddenly because none have been found after the very end of the Cretaceous Period. They also believe that they have proof that a meteorite caused the extinction because they have found some clay sediments that were deposited on the Earth just at the end of the Cretaceous Period which contain some very rare minerals including the element iridium at unusually high levels. This has been called the 'Iridium anomaly' by the scientists involved, and they claim that the only way that such high

The Reptile Family Tree (right)

Reptiles can be subdivided into four major groups on the basis of the pattern of openings in the back of the skull. These are anapsids, synapsids, diapsids and eurypsids (see drawings below and main headings on chart). Anapsids seem to be the most primitive types of reptile since they have no special skull openings and appear earliest in the fossil record. *Hylonomus* is one of the earliest definite reptiles; it comes from late Carboniferous deposits of Nova Scotia. The only surviving anapsids are the turtles and tortoises. Synapsids have an impressive fossil record. The earliest forms, pelycosaurs, appeared in the late Carboniferous and are followed by the therapsids and cynodonts of the Permian and Triassic. Synapsid reptiles went extinct in the late Triassic or early Jurassic, but gave rise to the earliest mammals which survived the reign of the dinosaurs and then evolved rapidly. Diapsids can be divided into two groups: lepidosaurs (lizards and snakes) and archosaurs (crocodiles, dinosaurs and their kin). The archosaurs date back to the late Permian proterosuchians which were followed by the late Triassic phytosaurs and true crocodiles. The Triassic was the time of origin of all major archosaur groups from the thecodontians to the aerial pterosaurs and the dinosaurs. Note that the birds are here related to theropod dinosaurs. Eurypsids are an uncertain group including the placodonts, ichthyosaurs, and plesiosaurs, all of which were swimming forms.

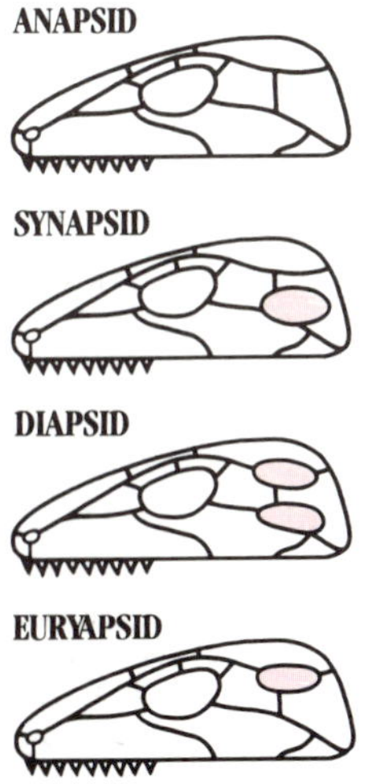

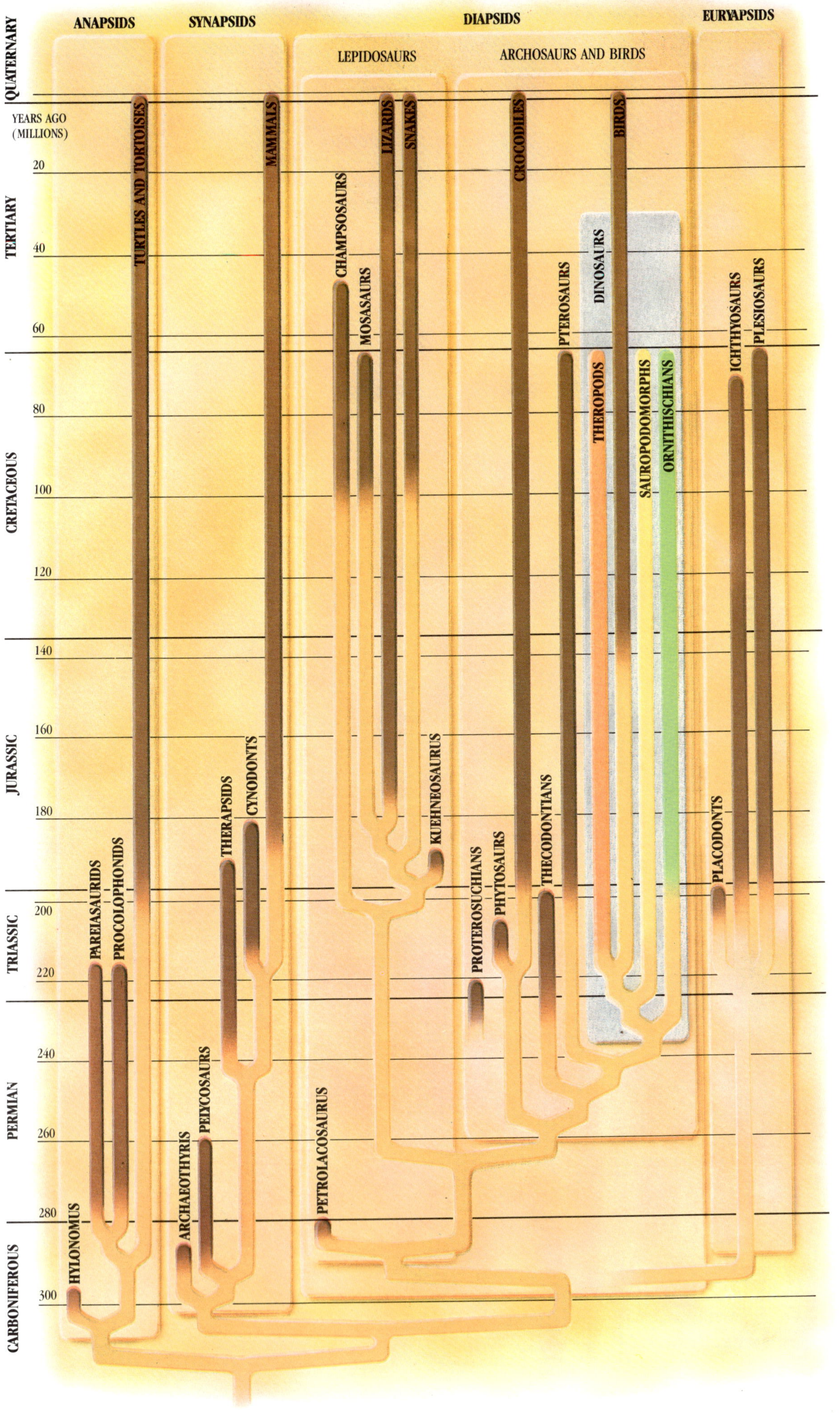

levels of Iridium could have got into these minerals is through a meteorite from outer space. The Iridium would have come from the dust of the meteorite as it exploded against the surface of the Earth like a huge bomb.

Convincing though this all sounds, there are still quite a few scientists who favour the weather change theory. They argue that the fossils show that the dinosaurs did not suddenly become extinct, as is claimed, but seem to have dwindled in type and variety over a period of several millions of years. They also show that the types of plant gradually change from warmth loving varieties to those that prefer a cooler climate. These scientists claim that the Iridium anomaly has nothing to do with a meteorite collision with the Earth but was caused by lots of volcanic activity towards the end of the Cretaceous Period. Iridium is trapped in the molten rocks at the centre of the Earth until it is thrown out during big volcanic eruptions.

As you can now appreciate, it is impossible to give a straightforward answer to the question: what killed the dinosaurs?

How much do we know about dinosaurs?

We can learn a great deal through very hard scientific study. By that I mean that we are able to build up a good idea about each dinosaur from a careful study of its fossilised remains. These can include things other than just their bones. For example, footprints, teeth and skin are sometimes preserved which can tell us a great deal about how and where they walked, what they ate, and what they looked like. The only thing that we really have to guess about is their colour.

Are dinosaurs really all extinct?

One last thought before leaving you to the delights of the dinosaurs that are awaiting you in this book; despite all that I have just said about dinosaurs being extinct, this may not be quite true! Birds seem to be such close relatives of dinosaurs, that you could almost say that dinosaurs live on today in a feathery disguise. Take a look at the legs and feet of a large bird like an ostrich or an emu, or even one of the birds in your garden. I wonder if those scaly legs and toes will remind you of anything that you are about to discover in this book?

Clothing in Muscles and Skin (above)
It is possible to clothe the skeleton of *Iguanodon* in the muscles of the shoulders, hips and head from the analysis so far given. Add to this the general muscles of the neck, belly and tail (middle picture) and we can wrap it in skin and provide a restoration of the animal as a living creature. (From Mark Hallett's drawings.)

Dinosaurs world-wide (right)
This map of the world shows the places where many of the dinosaurs that we know today have been found. As you can see they are found practically everywhere. More importantly, dinosaurs will certainly be found in areas not marked on this map; some have just been discovered in Alaska. Dinosaur footprints are also known in Korea and Spitzbergen, so their fossil remains should also be there.

The Dinosaur Family Tree (right)
The major division of the dinosaurs is into the *Saurischia* and *Ornithischia*; it is based primarily on the differences in hip structure (see page 4). The *Saurischia* are further subdivided into *Theropoda* and *Sauropodomorpha*. The theropods included a wide variety of carnivorous (meat-eating) dinosaurs all of which were *bipedal* (two-legged). They range from small fast runners such as 'coelurosaurs', to the larger 'carnosaurs' and tyrannosaurids of the late Cretaceous. The sauropodomorphs were the large plant-eating dinosaurs of the Mesozoic. They include the partially *bipedal* prosauropods of the late Triassic and early Jurassic and the massive *quadrupedal* (four-legged) sauropods of the later Jurassic and Cretaceous.

The *Ornithischia* were all *herbivores* (plant-eaters). They can be further divided into a series of distinctive types: *Ornithopoda*, *Ceratopia*, 'Pachycephalosaurs', *Stegosauria* and *Ankylosauria*. Ornithopods first appeared in the early Jurassic with small, lightly-built creatures such as the fabrosaurids. They culminate in the late Cretaceous hadrosaurids. Ceratopians were a late Cretaceous group characterised by peculiar parrot-like beaks, horns and frills. Pachycephalosaurs were a strange group with oddly thickened skulls, while the stegosaurs and ankylosaurs were distinctively armoured types.

As can be seen, the various family groups have been given distinctive coloured bands (keyed below). The length of the coloured 'fingers' in this diagram corresponds to the geological time range in which we have found members of the family group.

- THEROPODA
- SAUROPODOMORPHA
- ORNITHOPODA
- CERATOPIA
- 'PACHYCEPHALOSAURS'
- STEGOSAURIA
- ANKYLOSAURIA

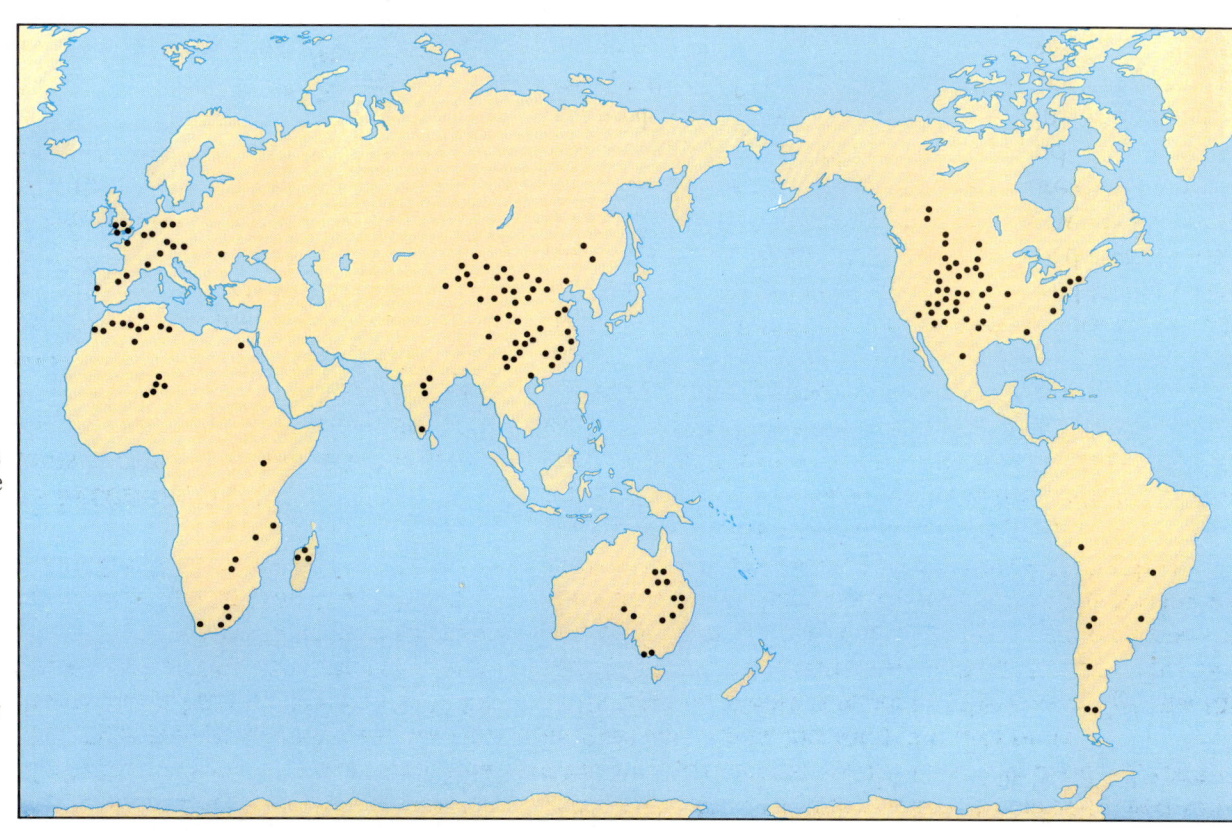

'COELUROSAURS'
From left to right: Compsognathus, Coelophysis, Ornitholestes

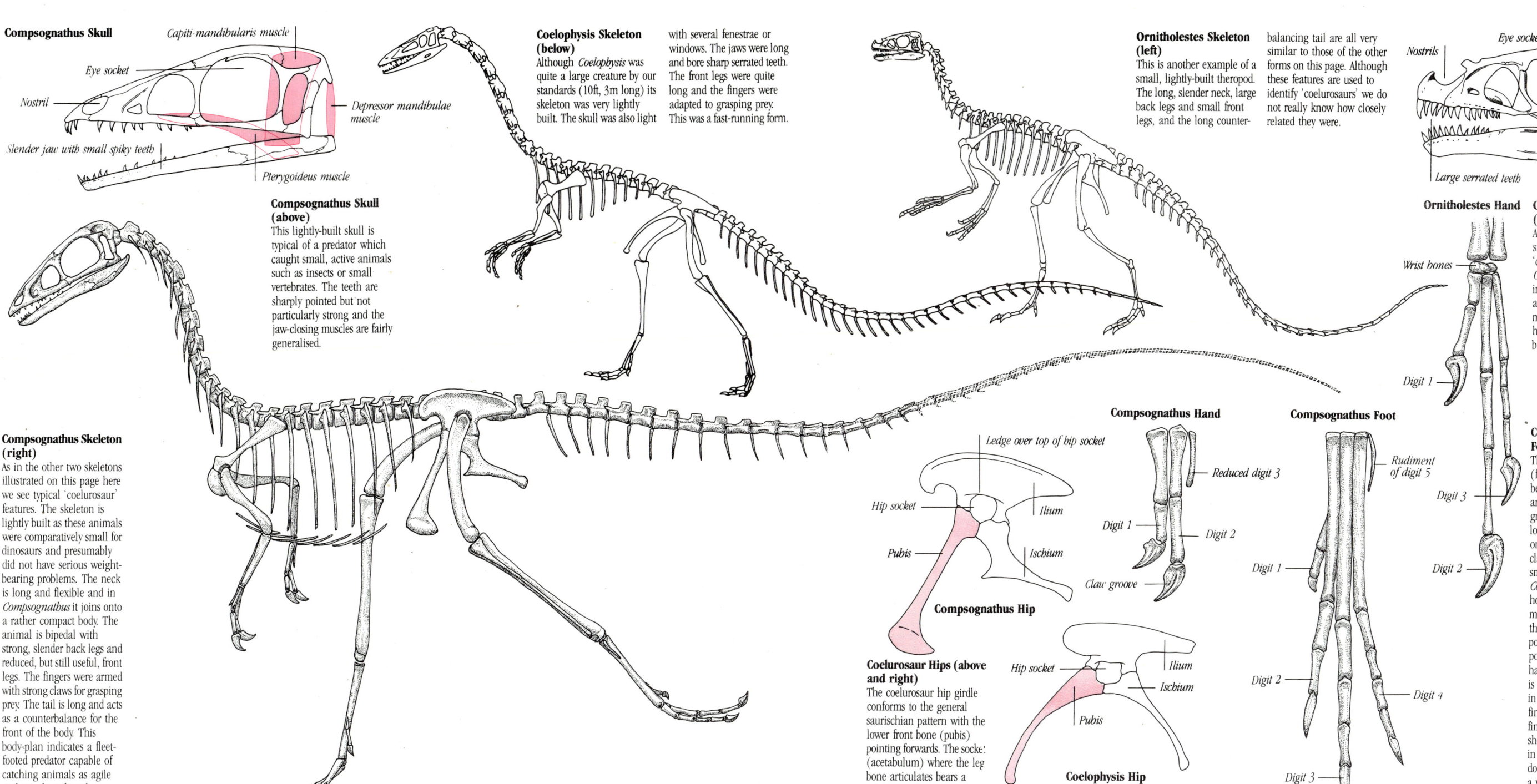

Compsognathus Skull
Nostril · Eye socket · Capiti-mandibularis muscle · Depressor mandibulae muscle · Slender jaw with small spiky teeth · Pterygoideus muscle

Compsognathus Skull (above)
This lightly-built skull is typical of a predator which caught small, active animals such as insects or small vertebrates. The teeth are sharply pointed but not particularly strong and the jaw-closing muscles are fairly generalised.

Coelophysis Skeleton (below)
Although *Coelophysis* was quite a large creature by our standards (10ft, 3m long) its skeleton was very lightly built. The skull was also light with several fenestrae or windows. The jaws were long and bore sharp serrated teeth. The front legs were quite long and the fingers were adapted to grasping prey. This was a fast-running form.

Ornitholestes Skeleton (left)
This is another example of a small, lightly-built theropod. The long, slender neck, large back legs and small front legs, and the long counter-balancing tail are all very similar to those of the other forms on this page. Although these features are used to identify 'coelurosaurs' we do not really know how closely related they were.

Ornitholestes Skull (above)
Nostrils · Eye socket · Large serrated teeth · Heavy jaw

Ornitholestes Hand
Wrist bones · Digit 1

Compsognathus Skeleton (right)
As in the other two skeletons illustrated on this page here we see typical 'coelurosaur' features. The skeleton is lightly built as these animals were comparatively small for dinosaurs and presumably did not have serious weight-bearing problems. The neck is long and flexible and in *Compsognathus* it joins onto a rather compact body. The animal is bipedal with strong, slender back legs and reduced, but still useful, front legs. The fingers were armed with strong claws for grasping prey. The tail is long and acts as a counterbalance for the front of the body. This body-plan indicates a fleet-footed predator capable of catching animals as agile and speedy as lizards.

Compsognathus Hip
Ledge over top of hip socket · Hip socket · Pubis · Ilium · Ischium

Coelurosaur Hips (above and right)
The coelurosaur hip girdle conforms to the general saurischian pattern with the lower front bone (pubis) pointing forwards. The socket (acetabulum) where the leg bone articulates bears a window or fenestra.

Coelophysis Hip
Hip socket · Pubis · Ilium · Ischium

Compsognathus Hand
Reduced digit 3 · Digit 1 · Digit 2 · Claw groove

Compsognathus Foot
Rudiment of digit 5 · Digit 1 · Digit 2 · Digit 3 · Digit 4

Coelurosaur Hands and Feet (left)
The hand of *Compsognathus* (far left) is rather peculiar in being so short, since an animal which presumably grasped its prey would need a longer hand to do so. Also only two of the fingers are clawed and the third is very small indeed. The foot of *Compsognathus* (middle left), however, is quite typical of most 'coelurosaurs' with three long, slender, forward-pointing toes and a fourth pointing backwards. The hand of *Ornitholestes* (left) is unusual for 'coelurosaurs' in having two especially long fingers and a short first finger. It is possible that this short finger could be turned in towards the others, as we do with our thumb, providing a very effective mechanism for gripping prey.

These are small, meat-eating theropod saurischian dinosaurs. The unusual name 'coelurosaur' means literally 'hollow-tailed reptile'. The name arose because some of the first bones of these animals ever recovered were, indeed, tail bones, and the broken ends of these revealed that they were hollow. This would have made them surprisingly light in real life.

Coelurosaurs are distinguished from the other theropod dinosaurs (see Introduction) only in very general terms as being small, slender and evidently agile creatures. For the most part, they have long slim legs and arms. Their hands are equipped with sharply taloned grasping claws, their necks are rather long and their heads tend to be rather small. The jaws are lined with lots of small, sharp teeth.

If we were to compare these sorts of animal with ones living today, the nearest equivalent might, perhaps, be the smaller cats and dogs which of course run on all four legs rather than on just two. Although cats/dogs and coelurosaurs do not look like one another very much in outward appearance, we do suspect that these two groups would have had rather similar ways of life: both being small, lightly built and agile they would be fierce, merciless killers of other creatures that were smaller than themselves.

Coelophysis (hollow form) is a well-known dinosaur from North America (New Mexico) where it was first discovered back in the 1880s. At first, as is usual for these sorts of dinosaur, only the odd rather scrappy remains were discovered. This was enough to tell scientists that these were the remains of a coelurosaur, but not much more than that. Much later, in the 1940s, scientists returned to the area in New Mexico where the first *Coelophysis* remains had been found and started to look again. This time they were really lucky. Not only did they find more of this dinosaur, they also came across what appears to have been a dinosaur graveyard. Lots and lots of dinosaur skeletons were discovered lying one on top of the other, and many of them were practically complete. As a result of this marvellous find, which included *Coelophysis* of all ages from very young to fully grown, we do know quite a lot about how this dinosaur looked.

Compsognathus (pretty jaw) comes from rocks in southern Germany and appears to have been much smaller than *Coelophysis*. One well preserved skeleton is no more than 28in (70cms) long. Again, the body of this creature is small and slender and it has a long, rather whippy tail. Apart from its comparatively small size, the only other feature of note are its arms which are very short for an animal that would use them to catch things with. The hands are small and only have two proper fingers—there is a third, but it was too little to have been of any use at all.

This dinosaur probably fed on insects and small lizards rather than anything bigger and stronger. In fact, the remains of a lizard have been found inside one skeleton of *Compsognathus*.

Ornitholestes (bird robber) comes from rocks in Wyoming. Although not as well preserved as the two animals described above, enough of it is known to allow us to piece together its appearance fairly accurately. The head is short and the teeth are large and sharp, which tells us that it would have had a very powerful bite. It would have been a fast runner, and it had very strong hands with three clawed fingers of different lengths. The short first finger could be swung in against the other two which gave it a particularly powerful grip.

Ornithomimosaurs & Oviraptorosaurs

From left to right: Struthiomimus, Oviraptor, Dromiceiomimus

Belly Ribs of Struthiomimus (below)
Belly ribs, or gastralia, are found in various reptile groups although they are absent from mammals. They are not formed in the same way as vertebral ribs and should not strictly be called by the same name. No-one really knows what their function is but there have been several suggestions. They may have been to support the abdomen, especially important in an herbivore with a large gut.

Struthiomimus Skeleton (right)
This skeleton is an odd mixture of rigidity and flexibility. The neck was long, slender and presumably highly mobile but the vertebrae of the back were held stiffly in place by strong ligaments. The end of the tail was also very stiff since the prongs of bone which joined the vertebrae together were very long and so restricted movement. The front legs were relatively long, and very slender.

Struthiomimus Skull (left)
The long slender, toothless jaw and large eyes give this skull a very bird-like appearance. It is also probable that the jaws were covered with horn. The lightness and thinness of the skull bones suggest that they may have been flexible, allowing movement in the skull, as in modern birds.

Dromiceiomimus Skull (right)
This is another lightly built ornithomimosaur skull. It is very similar to that of *Struthiomimus*. In fact, it is the body skeleton of *Dromiceiomimus* which really distinguishes it from other ornithomimosaurs: the short back, slender front leg, and slightly differently arranged pelvic bones. The eye socket is very large.

Oviraptor Skulls (right)
Several skulls belonging to this genus have been described and they exhibit quite a lot of variety. The top two skulls have been assigned to the species *philoceratops*, yet one has a small bump in the nasal region, while the other has a large crest. The third and fourth drawings show another species from Mongolia which has yet to be described. Its large eye sockets and smooth bone contours suggest that it is a juvenile animal.

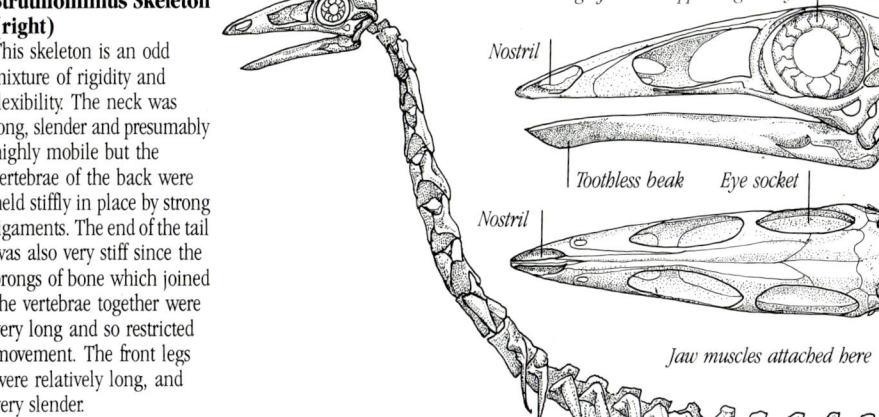
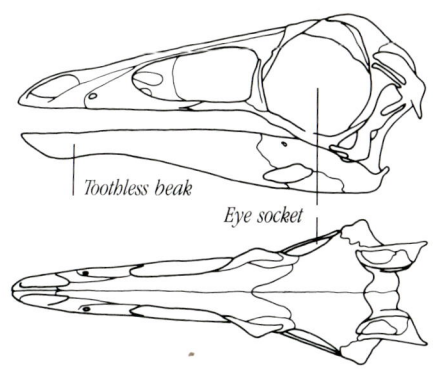
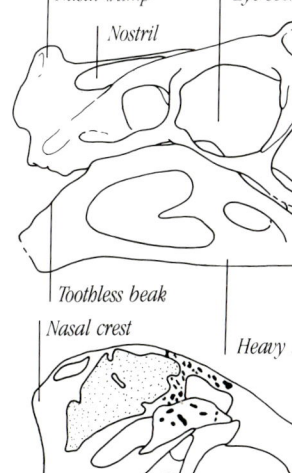

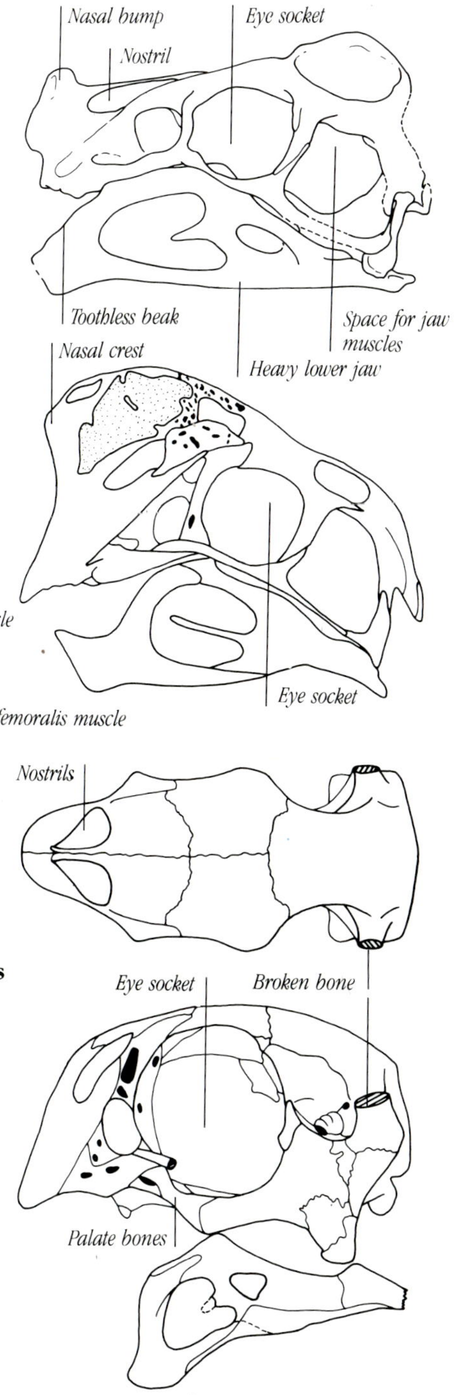

Gastralia

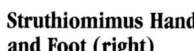

Struthiomimus Hand and Foot (right)
The foot (far right) provides evidence that *Struthiomimus* was a running creature. The toes are rather long and slender, but the upper foot bones (metatarsals) are very elongate. The foot bears an obvious resemblance to that of large running birds such as ostriches. The claws are narrow and flattened and may have provided traction with the ground to stop the foot slipping as it was thrust backwards during running. The hand is rather lightly built but looks as though it would form a useful gripping mechanism, perhaps for bending down the branches of trees, and so bringing them within range of *Struthiomimus'* slender toothless beak.

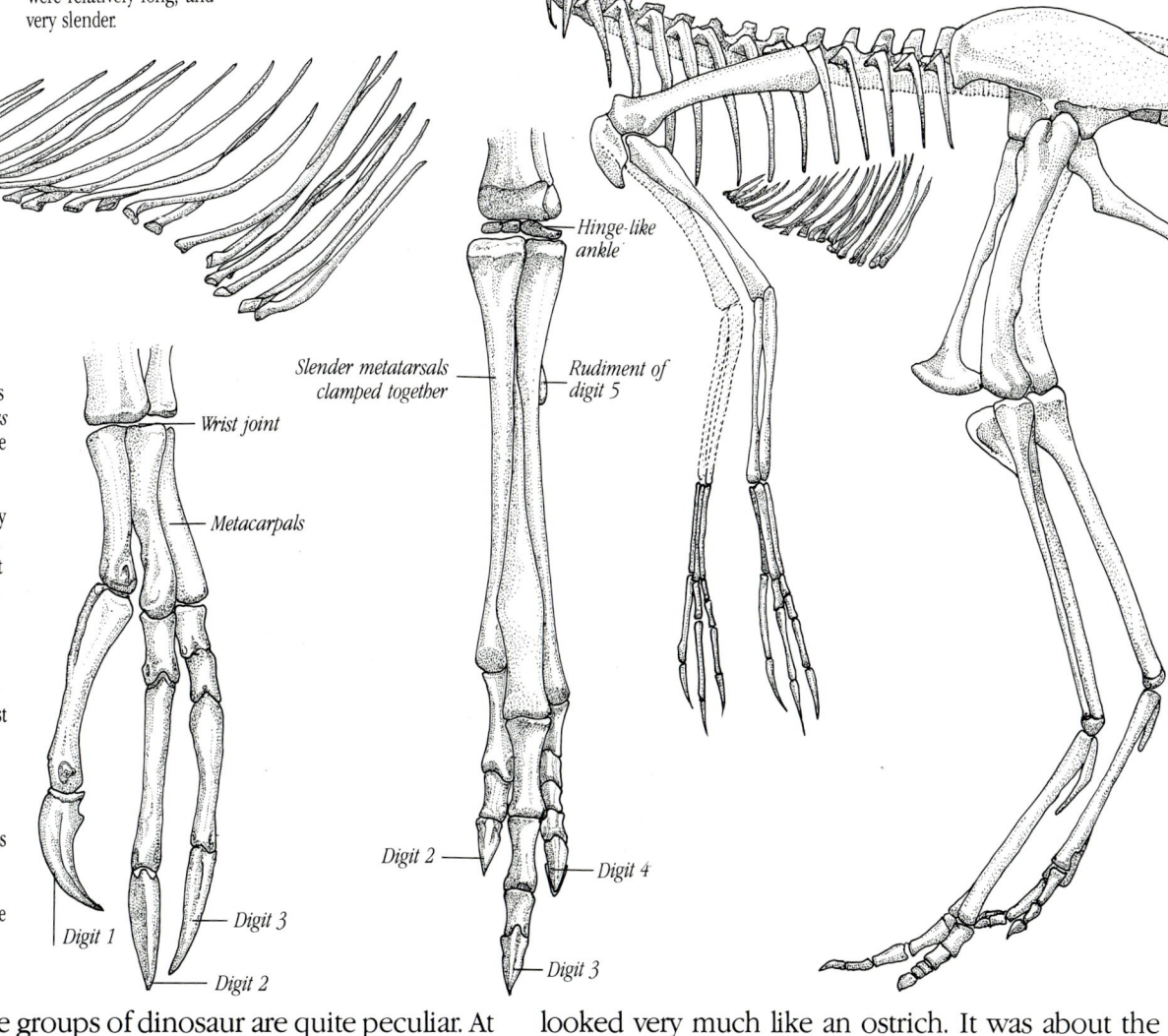

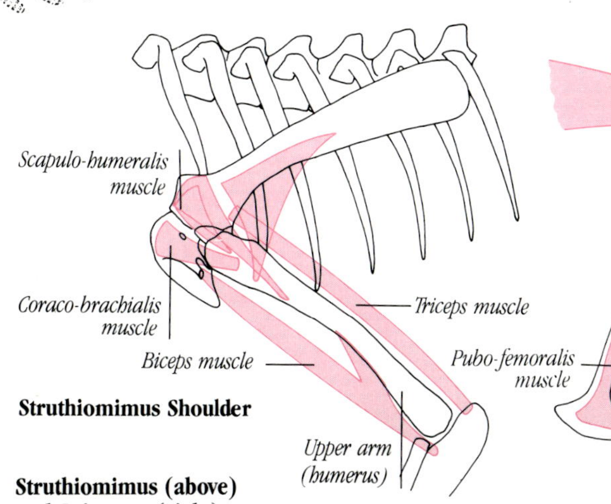

Struthiomimus Shoulder

Struthiomimus (above) and Oviraptor (right) Shoulders
The muscles reconstructed on the *Struthiomimus* shoulder are fairly generalised and would have permitted quite a wide range of movement. The shoulder girdle of *Oviraptor* shows that a collar bone is present in this theropod at least. It is shown in top view (near right) and in side view.

Oviraptor Shoulder

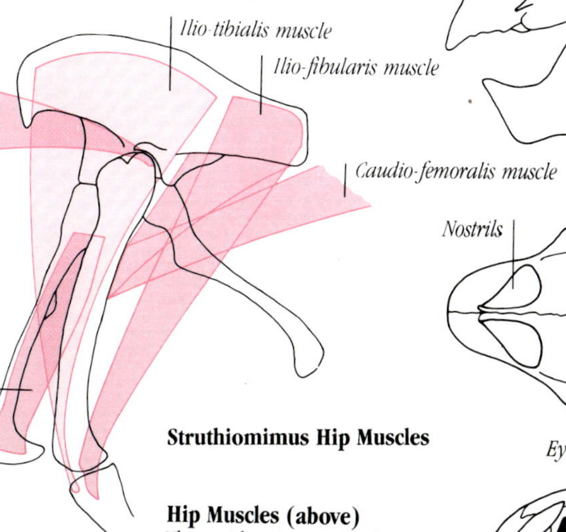

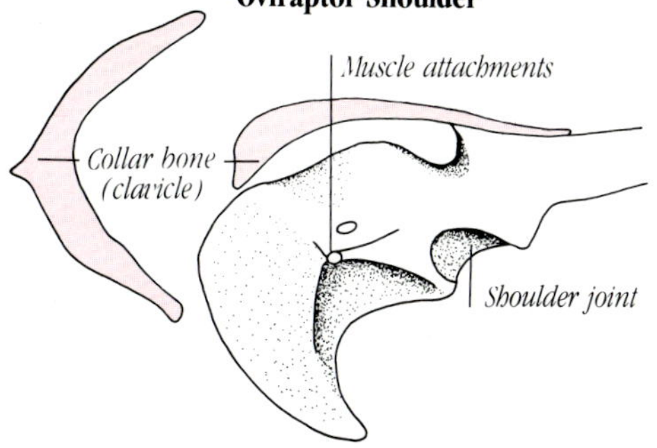

Struthiomimus Hip Muscles

Hip Muscles (above)
The ornithomimosaur back leg is built for speed, not weight-bearing, and this is reflected in the hip muscles. The main muscles responsible for the power-stroke action, as well as those for the recovery stroke, run from the girdle itself to the upper part of the leg. This high insertion produces a more rapid swing of the leg, and thus more speed.

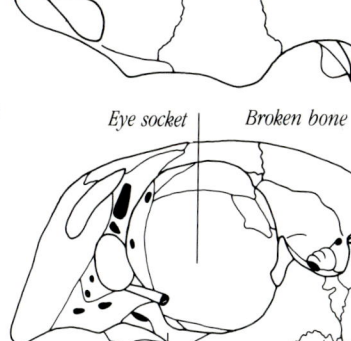

Both of these groups of dinosaur are quite peculiar. At first sight they look much like any other group of coelurosaurs, with spindly legs, long arms with grasping hands, long necks and small heads. However, they all share one quite extraordinary feature, which is that they do not have any teeth!

Ornithomimosaurs — the name means 'bird mimic reptile' — are also popularly known as 'ostrich dinosaurs' because, as you can see, they do look rather ostrich-like even though they do not have any feathers. These dinosaurs are known from rocks of late Cretaceous age. Their remains have been discovered in North America and Asia.

Struthiomimus (Ostrich mimic) was found as an almost complete skeleton. The only pieces missing were part of the head and a few bones from the rest of the body. Unlike anything that had been discovered before, this dinosaur looked very much like an ostrich. It was about the same size as an ostrich, had long legs, a short body, a long neck and a small, flat head. There are of course a few tell-tale differences such as a long, bony tail (birds only have a short 'parson's nose' from which the tail feathers sprout) and the long clawed hands (birds of course, even ostriches, have wings). The really unusual discovery was that, like the ostrich, this dinosaur did not have any teeth.

Apart from its head, the rest of the skeleton of this dinosaur was quite unusual. The neck was long and was evidently rather flexible, while its back was very stiff; the bones of the back were held in place by an arrangement of tight sinews, and the belly region was held stiff by a group of belly ribs (called gastralia). The tail was also stiffened toward its far end but was rather loose near the hips, so that it could be used for balance and for changing direction very quickly while running at speed. It seems quite likely that these dinosaurs lived very similarly to ostriches today.

Dromiceiomimus (Emu mimic) is another ornithomimosaur from Canada. It differs from *Struthiomimus* only very slightly in its body shape and the shape of its head.

Oviraptorosaurs (egg-stealing reptiles) are as peculiar as the ornithomimosaurs, if not more so. At the moment they are rather poorly known animals from Asia and possibly North America. The best known fossils of these animals come from Mongolia and were discovered in the 1920s by a famous expedition that went to Mongolia and discovered many skeletons and nests of the dinosaur *Protoceratops* (see pages 34-35). Amazingly, the skull of one of these dinosaurs was found lying on top of a nest of *Protoceratops* eggs as if it had died (or perhaps been killed by an enraged parent) in the act of stealing the eggs!

So far as we can tell from the remains that have so far been described, the bodies of these animals were much like that of most coelurosaurs, but the head is most remarkable. As with the ornithomimosaurs, there are no teeth in the mouth and the head is quite short and chunky with a variety of large lumps on it which are totally puzzling. New fossils have been discovered in the last few years in Mongolia which will no doubt help us to understand these animals much better.

Oviraptor (egg thief) was first discovered in Mongolia in the 1920s. Since then, a small, toothless skull, looking very much like that of the Mongolian *Oviraptor*, has been found in Canada. This indicates that these dinosaurs were also in North America at the end of the Cretaceous Period. As the name suggests *Oviraptor* may have fed on other dinosaurs' eggs.

DROMAEOSAURIDS
From left to right: Velociraptor, Deinonychus, Dromaeosaurus

Head (below and right)
Apart from the area around the jaws, where the teeth have to be firmly anchored in bone, the head of *Deinonychus* is composed of thin struts of bone which are arranged to make it both strong and light. The jaw muscles (1, 2 and 3) are confined to the back of the head and stretch down to the lower jaw. Muscle 1 (below) gives the jaw its powerful 'bite', while muscle 2 'snaps' the jaws shut quickly. Muscle 3 at the back of the head simply opens the jaws wide.

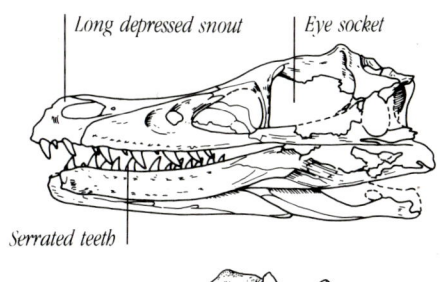

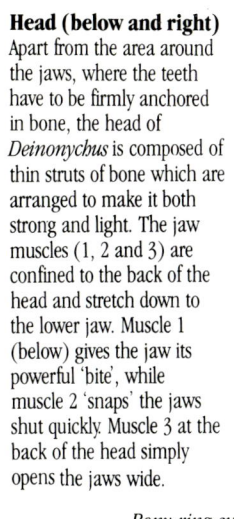

Velociraptor Skull (left)
This differs in shape from that of *Deinonychus*; it has a long, low, depressed snout. The eye sockets are large, and the irregular array of teeth are sharply serrated as one might expect in a carnivorous predator.

Arm and Shoulder (below)
This rather unusual diagram is drawn from a position looking down on the back of the animal from above its right shoulder. At the bottom are a row of vertebrae with part of the rib-cage, and the shoulder blade and arm in position. The shape and texture of the shoulder and arm bones show details of the shoulder muscles. Not surprisingly for an animal of this type which clutched its prey, the shoulders and arms were heavily muscled — some important muscles are illustrated in red.

Deinonychus Skeleton (below)
The colour restoration of *Deinonychus* on the opposite page is based on this detailed skeletal restoration. The large head is balanced on a slender, almost bird-like neck which was evidently very flexible. The chest was quite short and horizontal. The arms are shown held folded in their resting position against the flanks, rather like the wings of a bird at rest. The hip bones have been a matter of some controversy, especially the shape and size of the pubis. Early on, the pubis was not known at all, in fact a shoulder bone was accidentally put in its place! Now that the real pubis is known, its position is still not certain.

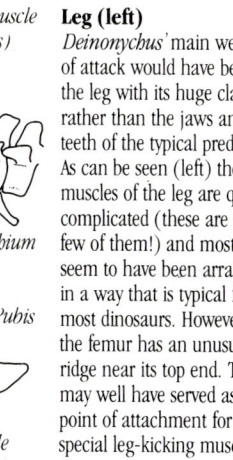

Leg (left)
Deinonychus' main weapon of attack would have been the leg with its huge claw, rather than the jaws and teeth of the typical predator. As can be seen (left) the muscles of the leg are quite complicated (these are just a few of them!) and most seem to have been arranged in a way that is typical for most dinosaurs. However, the femur has an unusual ridge near its top end. This may well have served as the point of attachment for a special leg-kicking muscle.

Tail (below)
As can be seen in the full skeleton (left) the part of the tail nearest the hips is quite normal in structure, with simple, block-like vertebrae. However, the remaining three-quarters of the tail is surrounded by a sheath of fine bony rods. As can be seen below, these rods are developed from each tail bone and served as muscle attachment sites and stiffeners. Muscles in the base of the tail attach to the bony rods so the tail may be held very still when running.

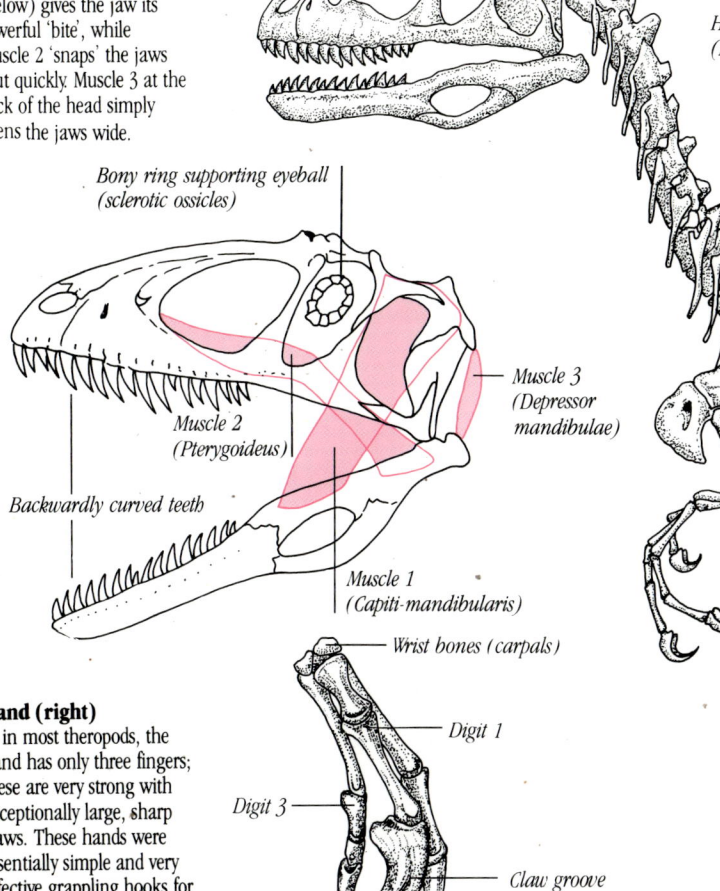

Hand (right)
As in most theropods, the hand has only three fingers; these are very strong with exceptionally large, sharp claws. These hands were essentially simple and very effective grappling hooks for holding on very tightly to prey. The small, pebble-like wrist bones are arranged so that the hand can be strongly flexed to improve grip.

The Foot and Claw (left)
The foot of *Deinonychus* is one of the most extraordinary of any dinosaur. As can be seen (left) it has four toes. The first toe is a small spur-like one, and very similar to the first toe of most theropods; it was probably held clear of the ground and may have been used for gripping food or prey. The second toe is the most striking feature of the foot, with its enormous claw. The joints of this toe are specially enlarged so that the toe can be raised upward and backward to avoid damage while running. The other two toes are of roughly equal length and were the only ones used for running upon. The toes could be flexed through a very wide arc (far left) to penetrate the flesh of the prey.

Dromaeosaurid dinosaurs were first discovered in North America in 1914. *Dromaeosaurus* (emu-like reptile) was the first dromaeosaurid to be found. It was a rather small creature no more than about 1.8m (6ft) long. The pieces that were found consisted of bits of the head and jaws and parts of the feet. These were very puzzling to the first scientists who looked at them, because, although they seemed to belong to a coelurosaur (pages 6-7), the animal had a rather large head, which is usually found in the bigger meat eating theropods such as the tyrannosaurids (pages 14-15).

Deinonychus (terrible claw) was a new dromaeosaurid found in 1964. Its remains were discovered in Montana and, in fact, several skeletons were found. It proved to be quite a bit larger than *Dromaeosaurus* — some of the largest skeletons reached about 3-4m (12-13 ft) in length.

As can be seen in the illustrations, *Deinonychus* was a fearsome animal. Just about every part of it is designed to make a terrible killing and butchering machine. Just like *Dromaeosaurus*, it had a very large head compared to its body and its long jaws were lined with big, curved, serrated teeth that enabled it to bite through skin very easily. Even though the head is big, the bones in it are surprisingly thin and there are large spaces for the muscles which give the jaws a very wide, strong bite. The arms are long, so that it would have had an excellent reach and they were very strong with powerful muscles to operate its sharp claws and give them a vicious grip.

The long legs are designed, as you would expect, for fast running to catch their prey. The remarkable thing about them is the foot. Even though *Deinonychus* has four toes on each of its feet, it actually runs and balances on just two of them on each foot. Of the other two, one is a small gripping toe which points backward, while the other is a huge slashing claw shaped like a sickle. The great big slashing claw which measured as much as 31cm (12in) is what gave *Deinonychus* its name.

The tail of *Deinonychus* is also unusual in that it is very stiff for most of its length, being held rigid by bony rods that lie alongside the tail bones. As we saw in the ornithomimosaurs (pages 8-9) a stiff tail can be very useful in aiding balance by counteracting the weight of the body and for changing direction when running fast.

So how did *Deinonychus* use all these bits and pieces when it was alive? Well, its large head with sharp teeth and long grabbing hands were obviously used to catch and eat its prey. What about that terrible claw? It is thought that the claw on the foot was used as a weapon as well; these animals probably jumped on to their prey and slashed at them with kicks from the feet that would have ripped their victim to pieces. The stiff tail would have helped *Deinonychus* to balance while it was doing this trick.

Velociraptor (speedy predator) is another dromaeosaurid dinosaur, but this one comes from Mongolia. The remains of this dinosaur were found in the 1920s but, again, these were far from complete, so little was known about it until more recently when more fossils were discovered.

One remarkable discovery of *Velociraptor* from Mongolia was made in the early 1970s. A complete skeleton of the animal was found in the rocks with its arms wrapped around the head of the skeleton of the small dinosaur *Protoceratops* (pages 34-35). This incredible find may show us one of those rare occasions when we can see the real combat between a predator and its prey.

'CARNOSAURS'
From left to right: Allosaurus, Ceratosaurus, Dilophosaurus

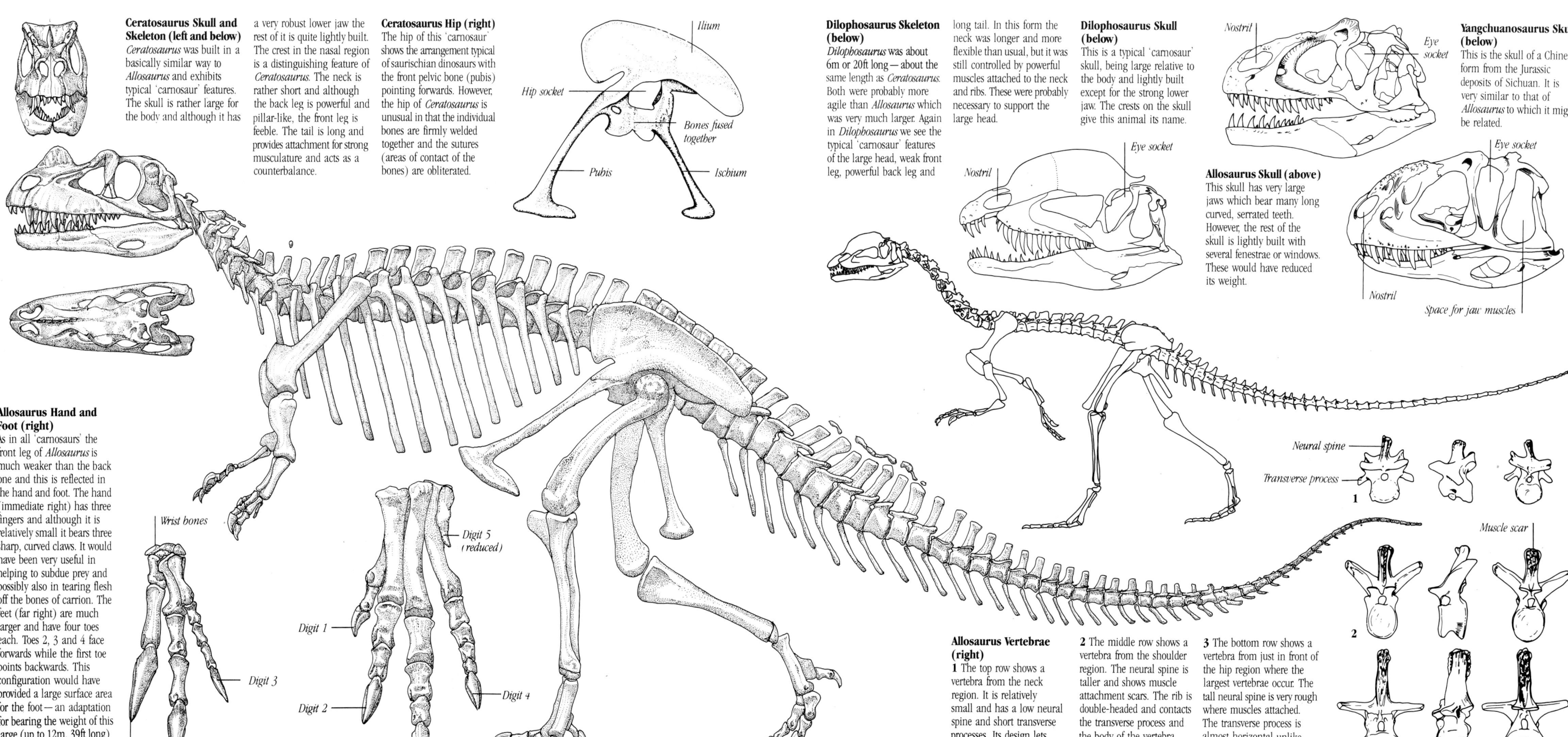

Ceratosaurus Skull and Skeleton (left and below)
Ceratosaurus was built in a basically similar way to *Allosaurus* and exhibits typical 'carnosaur' features. The skull is rather large for the body and although it has a very robust lower jaw the rest of it is quite lightly built. The crest in the nasal region is a distinguishing feature of *Ceratosaurus*. The neck is rather short and although the back leg is powerful and pillar-like, the front leg is feeble. The tail is long and provides attachment for strong musculature and acts as a counterbalance.

Ceratosaurus Hip (right)
The hip of this 'carnosaur' shows the arrangement typical of saurischian dinosaurs with the front pelvic bone (pubis) pointing forwards. However, the hip of *Ceratosaurus* is unusual in that the individual bones are firmly welded together and the sutures (areas of contact of the bones) are obliterated.

Dilophosaurus Skeleton (below)
Dilophosaurus was about 6m or 20ft long — about the same length as *Ceratosaurus*. Both were probably more agile than *Allosaurus* which was very much larger. Again in *Dilophosaurus* we see the typical 'carnosaur' features of the large head, weak front leg, powerful back leg and long tail. In this form the neck was longer and more flexible than usual, but it was still controlled by powerful muscles attached to the neck and ribs. These were probably necessary to support the large head.

Dilophosaurus Skull (below)
This is a typical 'carnosaur' skull, being large relative to the body and lightly built except for the strong lower jaw. The crests on the skull give this animal its name.

Allosaurus Skull (above)
This skull has very large jaws which bear many long curved, serrated teeth. However, the rest of the skull is lightly built with several fenestrae or windows. These would have reduced its weight.

Yangchuanosaurus Skull (below)
This is the skull of a Chinese form from the Jurassic deposits of Sichuan. It is very similar to that of *Allosaurus* to which it might be related.

Allosaurus Hand and Foot (right)
As in all 'carnosaurs' the front leg of *Allosaurus* is much weaker than the back one and this is reflected in the hand and foot. The hand (immediate right) has three fingers and although it is relatively small it bears three sharp, curved claws. It would have been very useful in helping to subdue prey and possibly also in tearing flesh off the bones of carrion. The feet (far right) are much larger and have four toes each. Toes 2, 3 and 4 face forwards while the first toe points backwards. This configuration would have provided a large surface area for the foot — an adaptation for bearing the weight of this large (up to 12m, 39ft long) lumbering theropod.

Allosaurus Vertebrae (right)
1 The top row shows a vertebra from the neck region. It is relatively small and has a low neural spine and short transverse processes. Its design lets the neck move freely.
2 The middle row shows a vertebra from the shoulder region. The neural spine is taller and shows muscle attachment scars. The rib is double-headed and contacts the transverse process and the body of the vertebra itself.
3 The bottom row shows a vertebra from just in front of the hip region where the largest vertebrae occur. The tall neural spine is very rough where muscles attached. The transverse process is almost horizontal unlike that of the shoulder.

These are a variety of large, meat-eating (theropod) dinosaurs. They have many common features and, like the coelurosaurs (pages 6-7) tend to look rather similar at first sight. All are 5m (15ft) or more in length and have large heads, short powerful necks, quite short but powerful arms, large legs and long tails. I suppose that these were the lions of the dinosaur world and would have preyed upon the larger plant eating dinosaurs and perhaps also scavenged the carcasses of dead creatures.

Fossil remains of carnosaurs have been found all over the world and throughout the time when dinosaurs are known to have lived on Earth (140 million years). Illustrated above are some of the best known carnosaurs: *Allosaurus*, *Ceratosaurus* and *Dilophosaurus*.

Allosaurus (strange reptile) was first found in rocks in Colorado, but it is now better known from Utah and Wyoming. It is a large carnosaur which is known to have reached lengths of 12m (39ft). In the past it also had another name *Antrodemus*, which you may have seen in some older books, but this is not now used.

The skull of *Allosaurus* is very large. It can be up to 1m (3.5ft) long and looks quite heavy with huge, curved, dagger-like teeth in its jaws. The mouth could be opened very wide so that great lumps of meat could be bolted down. One unusual thing about the head is that there is a large lump of bone over each eye, which makes them look as though they have got permanently raised eyebrows. Quite what this was for we do not really know, but it is possible that it was a special marker enabling individual *Allosaurus* to recognise one another; quite a lot of dinosaurs have odd bumps or ridges on their heads that can have had no purpose that we can think of unless it was to help them to recognise one another in the same way that birds use their brightly coloured feathers.

Apart from the head, the rest of the body is much as we have seen with all the different theropod groups described. The arms are rather short but have powerful talons on the hands. All the other groups of theropod that we have looked at so far have long arms for grabbing their prey. Carnosaurs like this seem to just use the arms for holding on to the prey once it has been bitten by those enormous jaws.

Ceratosaurus (horned reptile) also comes from Colorado, but although it lived at the same time as *Allosaurus*, it was quite a lot smaller. The largest specimens seem to have been about 6m (20ft) long. In its shape, *Ceratosaurus* is quite similar to *Allosaurus*, the one really obvious difference is on the head. *Ceratosaurus*, as its name tells us, has a horn on its nose as well as the ridges over its eyes that we saw in *Allosaurus*. Looking carefully at the hand you may also notice that *Ceratosaurus* has four fingers, while *Allosaurus* has only three.

Ceratosaurus fossils are rarely found in rocks while *Allosaurus* remains seem to be quite abundant. Does this tell us anything about the way of life of these creatures? Well it may. *Allosaurus* may have been a pack hunter, living in groups, rather like a pride of lions, while *Ceratosaurus* may have been a solitary hunter like the leopard, which may explain why its remains are so rare.

Dilophosaurus (two-ridged reptile) comes from the early Jurassic rocks of Arizona. It grew up to 6m (20ft) long and, again, has the same sort of body shape as the previous two examples. The main distinguishing mark of *Dilophosaurus* is the double ridge of bone on its head.

Tyrannosaurids

From left to right: Daspletosaurus, Albertosaurus, Tyrannosaurus

Tarbosaurus Skull (below)
This skull was very powerfully built, possibly to withstand the impact caused when the animal hurtled into its prey. Flexible areas in the skull may have absorbed some of the shock of the impact. The muscles would produce a powerful bite.

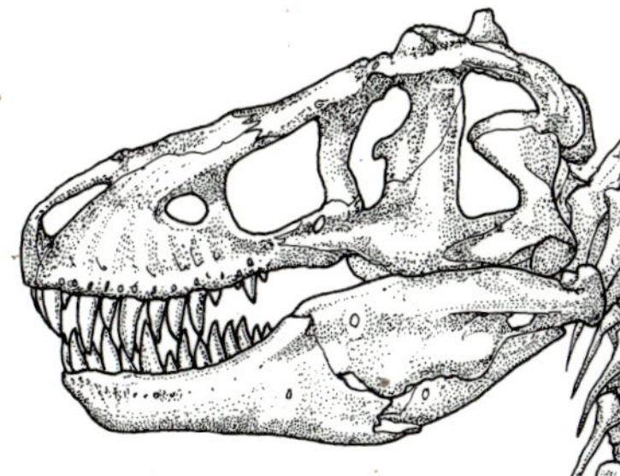

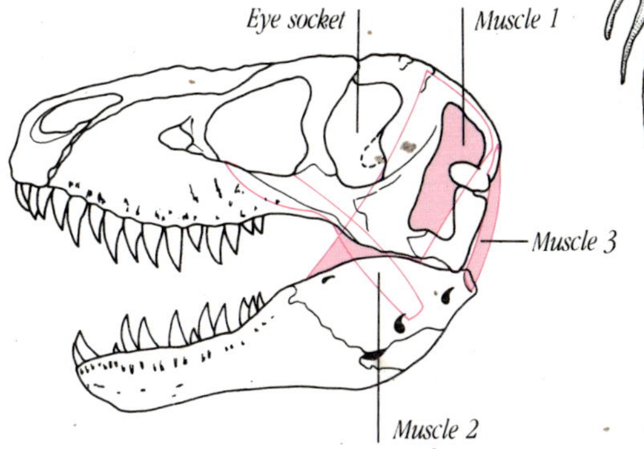

Tyrannosaurus Skeleton (below)
Tyrannosaurus was over 12.3m (40ft) long and might have weighed up to 7 tonnes, so its skeleton is a compromise between the need to bear this massive weight and to run around to catch food. The skull is much more massive than that of the 'carnosaurs' described earlier, built to withstand impact. It is supported by a stout neck which joins the compact back region. The bodies of the individual vertebrae are designed to withstand compression forces, while the stout ribs, joined by ligaments and muscles, would withstand tension. The hip girdle and back limb were extremely strong since they would take the animal's weight. The front legs were very small and feeble. The belly is lined with ribs—gastralia—which probably served to stiffen this area.

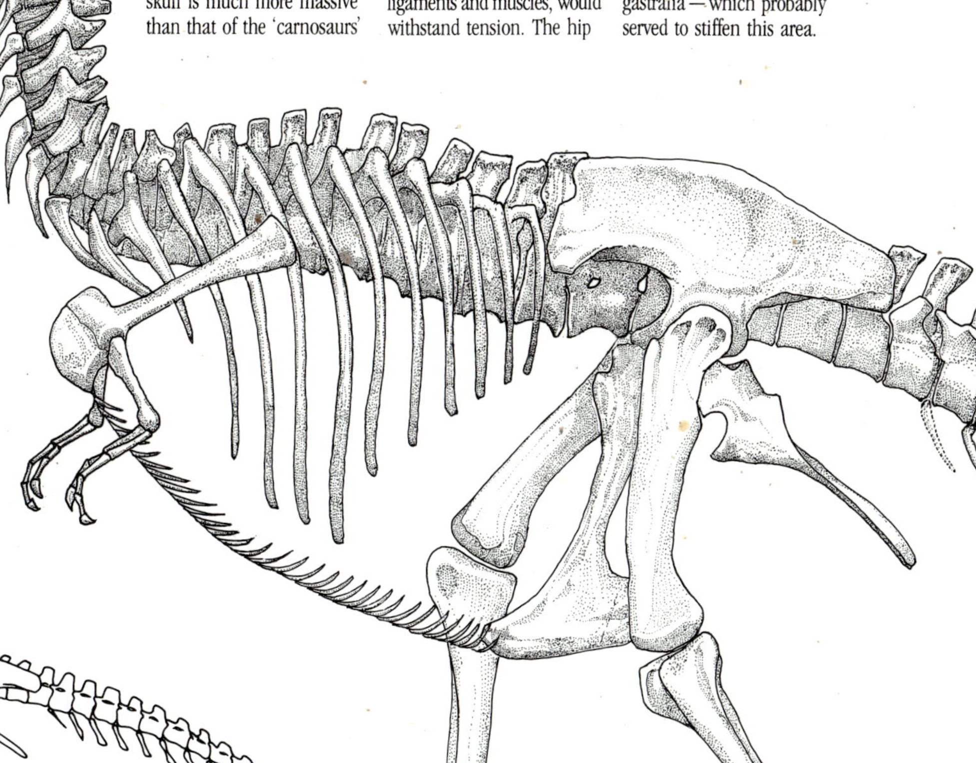

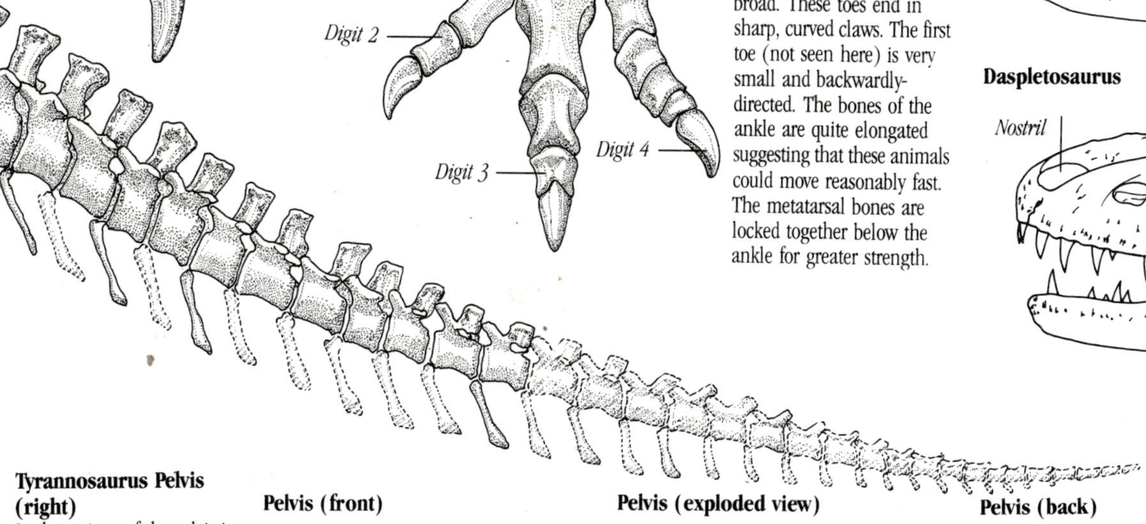

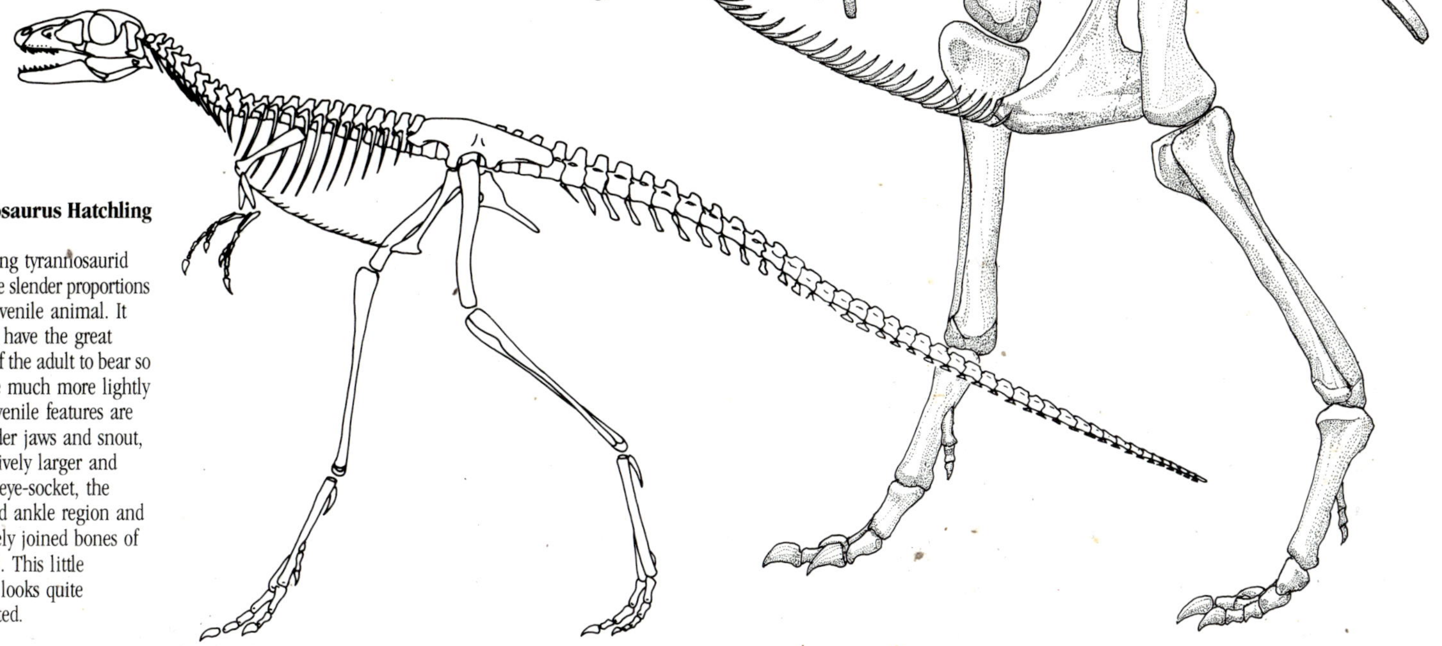

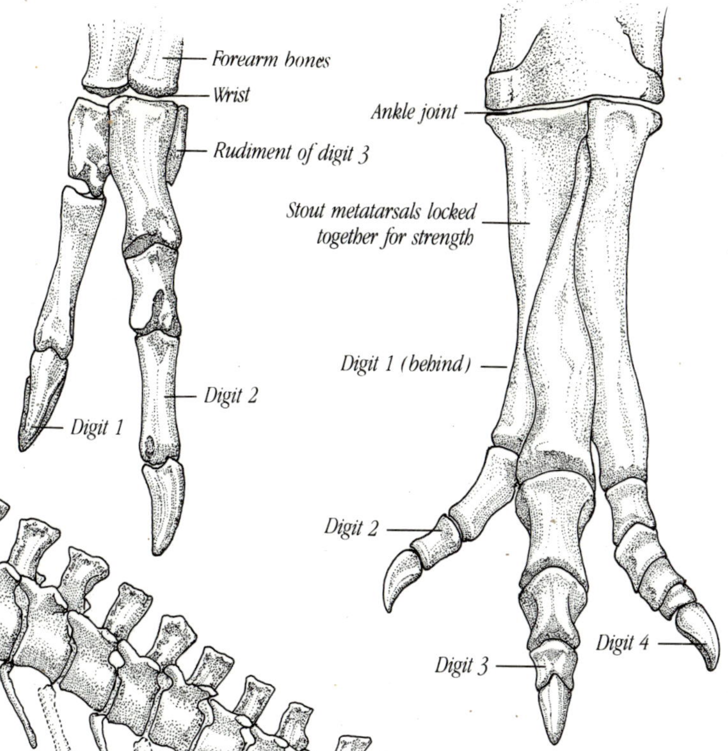

Tarbosaurus Hand and Foot (left)
The front leg is very small and ends in a feeble, two-fingered hand (far left). Each finger bears a stout claw, and it has been suggested that the hand might have been used as a kind of grappling hook during mating, or to anchor the front of the body as the animal tried to raise itself after resting on the ground. The foot is much stronger since the back leg takes the animal's weight. The three forwardly-pointing toes are quite short, but the foot is broad. These toes end in sharp, curved claws. The first toe (not seen here) is very small and backwardly-directed. The bones of the ankle are quite elongated suggesting that these animals could move reasonably fast. The metatarsal bones are locked together below the ankle for greater strength.

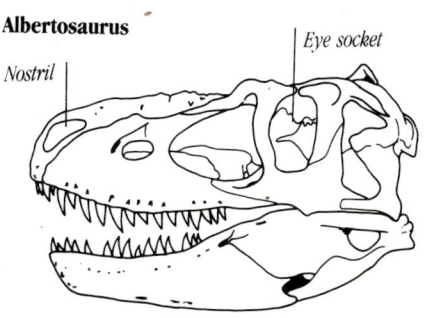
Albertosaurus

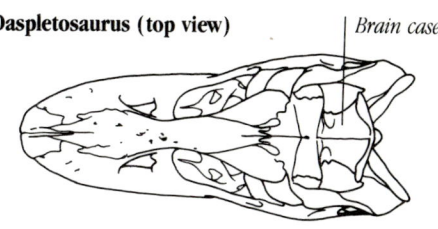
Daspletosaurus (top view)

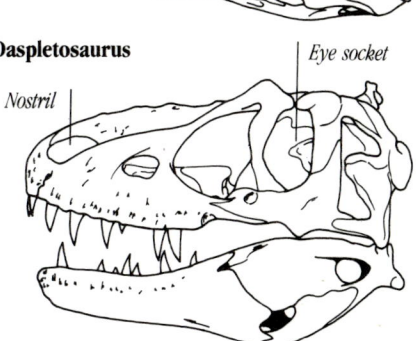
Daspletosaurus

Albertosaurus Hatchling (right)
This young tyrannosaurid shows the slender proportions of the juvenile animal. It does not have the great weight of the adult to bear so it can be much more lightly built. Juvenile features are the slender jaws and snout, the relatively larger and rounder eye-socket, the elongated ankle region and the loosely joined bones of the skull. This little creature looks quite fleet-footed.

Tyrannosaurus Pelvis (right)
In these views of the pelvis it is possible to see the upper pelvic bone (ilium) and the vertebrae which attach to it (sacral vertebrae). The lower pelvic bones are not shown. In the exploded view of the pelvis (middle, top and bottom) the wide, plate-like nature of the ilium is seen. This gives plenty of area for muscle attachment. The sockets for the sacral ribs (arrowed) are also visible in the middle drawing.

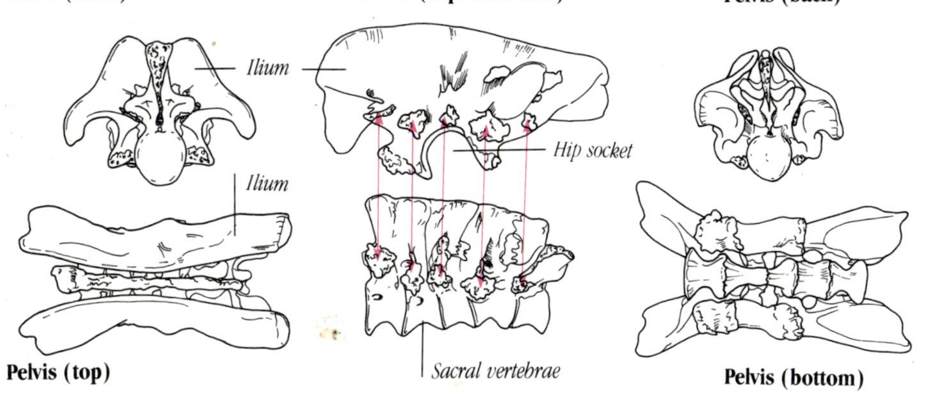

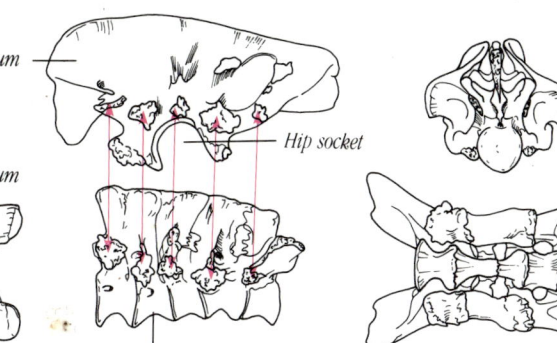

Tyrannosaurid Skulls (above)
The skull of *Albertosaurus* (top) is very similar to that of *Tyrannosaurus*. It is massively built with smaller skull windows surrounded by thicker struts of bone. The teeth are sharp and recurved (pointing backwards), typical of a carnivore. *Daspletosaurus* (middle and bottom) also has the typical tyrannosaurid build. It is distinguished by its teeth which, although fewer in number, are particularly large. All tyrannosaurid skulls show marked similarities.

These are, without doubt, the best known of all dinosaurs because they are the biggest—up to 14m (46ft) in length—and undoubtedly the most fearsome of all the dinosaurs. The fossil remains of tyrannosaurids have been found in North America and Asia and they seem to have lived during the late Cretaceous Period at the very end of the reign of the dinosaurs.

The first remains of tyrannosaurids were discovered towards the end of the last century. Unfortunately they were not recognised as being anything particularly special because these fossils were just broken fragments rather than well preserved skeletons. However, in 1902, a well preserved skeleton was discovered in Montana and more in Wyoming shortly after that. This material was named *Tyrannosaurus*, which became the name for the whole group of dinosaurs of this type. The ones that are best known are: *Tyrannosaurus, Albertosaurus, Daspletosaurus* and *Tarbosaurus*.

Tyrannosaurus (Tyrant reptile) which grew to as much as 14m (46ft) in total length was the largest of the known tyrannosaurids and must have been a truly terrifying animal. The skull of this animal was 1.3m (4ft) long and was very heavy with huge jaws lined with teeth that were up to 30cm (1ft) long. The edges of the teeth were notched like the edges of steak knives so that they could slice through the flesh of the animals that they were eating with the greatest of ease. The body of *Tyrannosaurus* was also very large and heavy. Its neck was thick and strong to support the huge head, and the back and tail were held quite stiffly. The back legs were long and strong to support the enormous weight of the body, and the feet were distinctly bird-like, with three large forward-pointing toes.

There are a few peculiar features of *Tyrannosaurus* that should be mentioned. Belly ribs can be seen very clearly on the skeleton. These helped to strengthen the back and the chest and may also have supported the belly when these animals were resting. This can be tied in with the large flat piece of bone between the knees of the skeleton, which also helped to support the belly and prevent the weight of the animal from crushing its insides as it lay down to rest.

The most absurd of all the features of the *Tyrannosaurus*, and all other tyrannosaurids for that matter, is the ridiculously small size of its arms and hands. We saw that in the carnosaurs the arms were rather small even though they were quite powerful, but tyrannosaurids have hands ending with two very small claws that do not even seem to be able to reach the mouth. It is thought that the hands were used as anchors, gripping on to the ground when the animal wanted to get up after resting. This would enable the *tyrannosaurus* to straighten its back legs without slipping forward on to its nose.

Albertosaurus (reptile from Alberta) was smaller than *Tyrannosaurus* reaching a length of 9m (29ft) and was more lightly built. It may have been a fairly swift hunter of smaller plant eaters such as hadrosaurids (pages 30-33).

Daspletosaurus (frightful flesh eating reptile) also from Alberta, was about the same size as *Albertosaurus*, but was more heavily built and may well have preferred to prey upon ceratopids (pages 36-39).

Tarbosaurus (reptile from Mongolia) was the Asian equivalent of the North American *Tyrannosaurus*. Its remains were discovered in the Gobi Desert in Mongolia. It was just as big and just as fierce as the *Tyrannosaurus* even though its head was a slightly different shape.

Prosauropods
Plateosaurus (left) and Anchisaurus

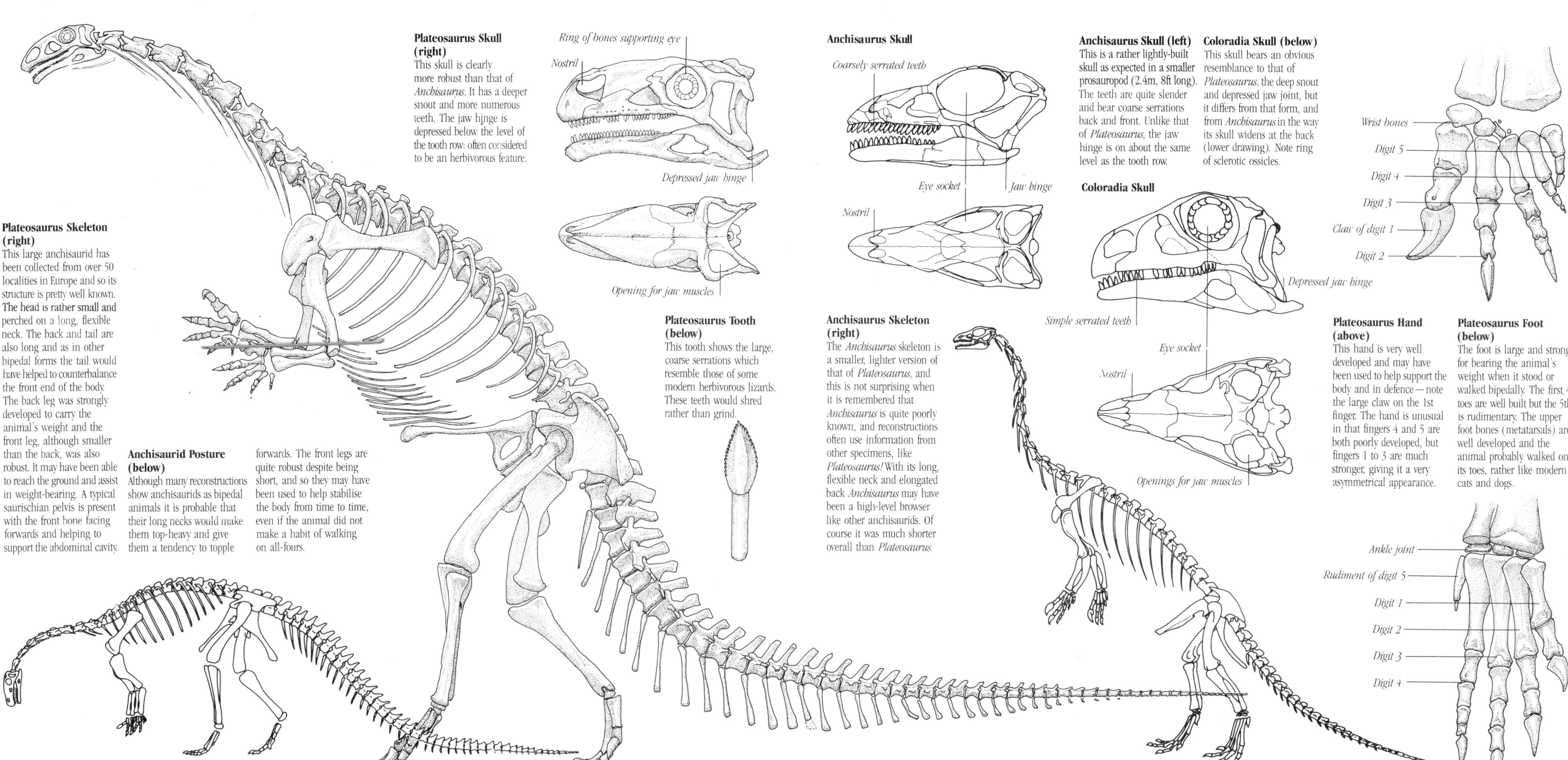

Plateosaurus Skeleton (right)
This large anchisaurid has been collected from over 50 localities in Europe and so its structure is pretty well known. The head is rather small and perched on a long, flexible neck. The back and tail are also long and as in other bipedal forms the tail would have helped to counterbalance the front end of the body. The back leg was strongly developed to carry the animal's weight and the front leg, although smaller than the back, was also robust. It may have been able to reach the ground and assist in weight-bearing. A typical saurischian pelvis is present with the front bone facing forwards and helping to support the abdominal cavity.

Anchisaurid Posture (below)
Although many reconstructions show anchisaurids as bipedal animals it is probable that their long necks would make them top-heavy and give them a tendency to topple forwards. The front legs are quite robust despite being short, and so they may have been used to help stabilise the body from time to time, even if the animal did not make a habit of walking on all-fours.

Plateosaurus Skull (right)
This skull is clearly more robust than that of *Anchisaurus*. It has a deeper snout and more numerous teeth. The jaw hinge is depressed below the level of the tooth row: often considered to be an herbivorous feature.

Plateosaurus Tooth (below)
This tooth shows the large, coarse serrations which resemble those of some modern herbivorous lizards. These teeth would shred rather than grind.

Anchisaurus Skeleton (right)
The *Anchisaurus* skeleton is a smaller, lighter version of that of *Plateosaurus*, and this is not surprising when it is remembered that *Anchisaurus* is quite poorly known, and reconstructions often use information from other specimens, like *Plateosaurus*! With its long, flexible neck and elongated back *Anchisaurus* may have been a high-level browser like other anchisaurids. Of course it was much shorter overall than *Plateosaurus*.

Anchisaurus Skull

Anchisaurus Skull (left)
This is a rather lightly-built skull as expected in a smaller prosauropod (2.4m, 8ft long). The teeth are quite slender and bear coarse serrations back and front. Unlike that of *Plateosaurus*, the jaw hinge is on about the same level as the tooth row.

Coloradia Skull (below)
This skull bears an obvious resemblance to that of *Plateosaurus*, the deep snout and depressed jaw joint, but it differs from that form, and from *Anchisaurus* in the way its skull widens at the back (lower drawing). Note ring of sclerotic ossicles.

Coloradia Skull

Plateosaurus Hand (above)
This hand is very well developed and may have been used to help support the body and in defence — note the large claw on the 1st finger. The hand is unusual in that fingers 4 and 5 are both poorly developed, but fingers 1 to 3 are much stronger, giving it a very asymmetrical appearance.

Plateosaurus Foot (below)
The foot is large and strong for bearing the animal's weight when it stood or walked bipedally. The first 4 toes are well built but the 5th is rudimentary. The upper foot bones (metatarsals) are well developed and the animal probably walked on its toes, rather like modern cats and dogs.

Prosauropods are the earliest known of the sauropodomorph dinosaurs. These are plant eating types of saurischian dinosaurs, unlike the meat eating theropods which we have been looking at over the last few pages. These dinosaurs are known from rocks on the late Triassic and early Jurassic age and are found practically worldwide. In fact, the only place that they have not been discovered to date is Antarctica. Unlike the meat eating theropods, the fossils of these dinosaurs are quite numerous whenever they are found.

Anchisaurus (close reptile) was discovered in 1818 in the Connecticut Valley of North America. Although it is perhaps a little small compared to most prosauropods, its appearance is still very typical. *Anchisaurus* grew to a length of about 2.5m (8ft) and was a rather slenderly built creature with a small pointed head, a fairly long neck and a long body and tail. Its back legs were strong and its front ones were shorter and had powerfully clawed hands similar to those of the theropods. The first three fingers had especially large talons.

How do we know that these animals were plant eaters? Well the answer is quite simple; we look at the shape of their teeth. Prosauropods all have the same type of teeth, which are shaped so that they look like a beech leaf (see the picture above). These sorts of teeth have a row of large ridges down each edge which look a little bit like the teeth on a saw blade. The ridges make them very rough when they rub past one another, enabling the dinosaur to shred up tough pieces of plant before swallowing them. The fact that they are plant eaters also explains why these animals tend to be rather long-bodied compared to the theropods. Plant eaters find all plants very difficult to digest and have to store the food that they have eaten in their stomachs for a very long time so that they can get all the goodness out of it. You can see that this is just as true today because nearly all plant eating animals such as elephants, cows, sheep and horses, are large and have large bellies. Even small plant eaters such as rabbits and mice have surprisingly large stomachs for their size.

Plateosaurus (flat reptile) is another well known prosauropod, but this one comes from Europe (France, East and West Germany, and Switzerland). Again, its remains were first found a long time ago back in the 1830s, but it was not really known in much detail until the early part of this century. It is particularly well known in Europe because at one place near the town of Trossingen in West Germany, a great collection of complete and partial skeletons of this animal were discovered.

As you can see, *Plateosaurus* grew much larger than *Anchisaurus*; some of the largest ones were as much as 10m (33ft) long. Apart from its much larger size, there is not really a lot of difference between *Plateosaurus* and *Anchisaurus*. The head is the most distinctive feature of the *Plateosaurus* having a much deeper snout, smaller eyes and many more smaller teeth. To make up for the fact that prosauropods have large bellies, they tend to have long tails so that the weight of the body was more or less balanced at the hips. The advantage of this sort of arrangement is that they could walk either on their back legs, as a theropod does, or on all four legs.

South America also has its share of prosauropods, such as *Coloradia* and, very interestingly, a tiny fossil prosauropod named *Mussaurus* (mouse reptile) whose whole skeleton can sit on the palm of your hand.

DIPLODOCIDS
Apatosaurus (left) and Diplodocus

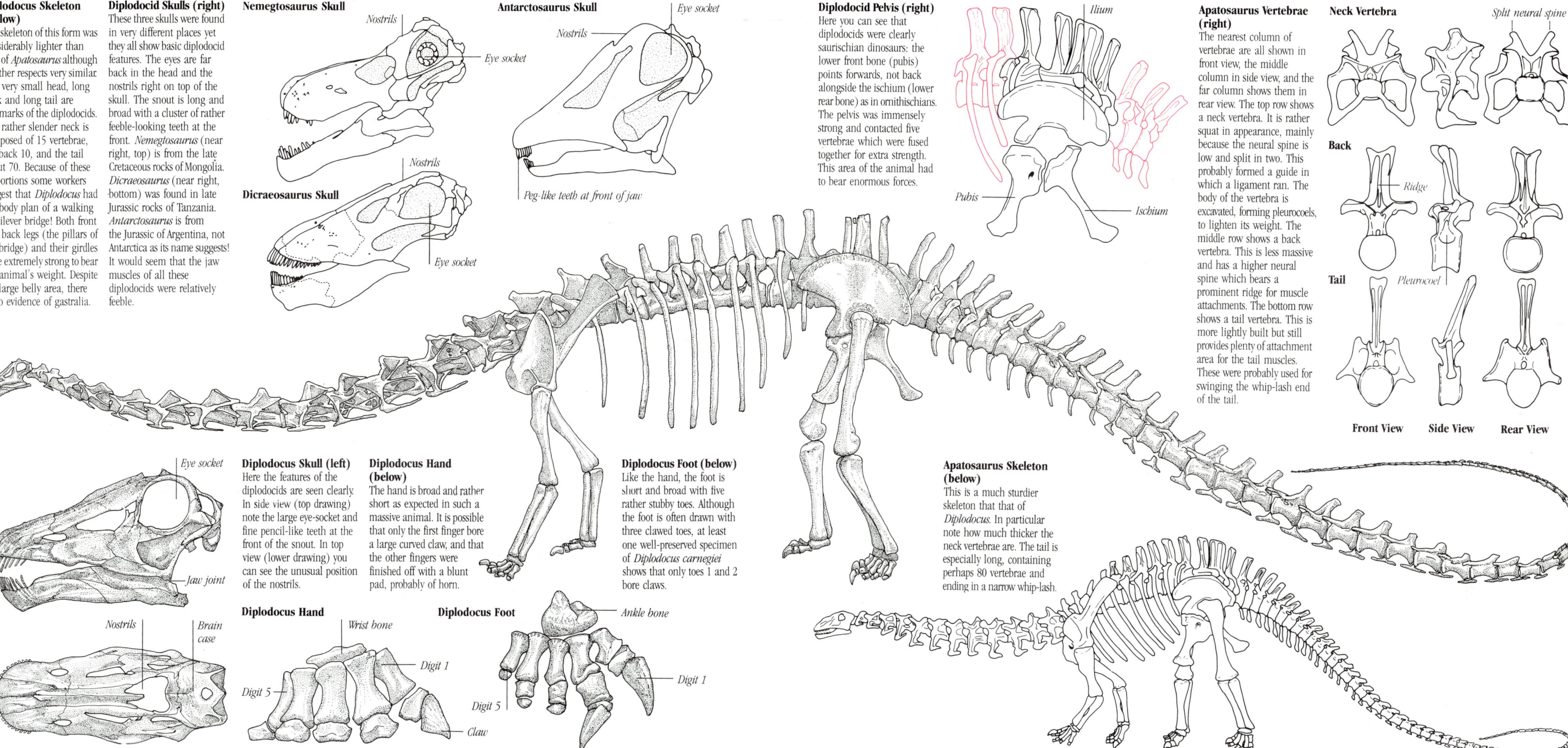

Diplodocus Skeleton (below) The skeleton of this form was considerably lighter than that of *Apatosaurus* although in other respects very similar. The very small head, long neck and long tail are hallmarks of the diplodocids. The rather slender neck is composed of 15 vertebrae, the back 10, and the tail about 70. Because of these proportions some workers suggest that *Diplodocus* had the body plan of a walking cantilever bridge! Both front and back legs (the pillars of the bridge) and their girdles were extremely strong to bear the animal's weight. Despite the large belly area, there is no evidence of gastralia.

Diplodocid Skulls (right) These three skulls were found in very different places yet they all show basic diplodocid features. The eyes are far back in the head and the nostrils right on top of the skull. The snout is long and broad with a cluster of rather feeble-looking teeth at the front. *Nemegtosaurus* (near right, top) is from the late Cretaceous rocks of Mongolia. *Dicraeosaurus* (near right, bottom) was found in late Jurassic rocks of Tanzania. *Antarctosaurus* is from the Jurassic of Argentina, not Antarctica as its name suggests! It would seem that the jaw muscles of all these diplodocids were relatively feeble.

Diplodocid Pelvis (right) Here you can see that diplodocids were clearly saurischian dinosaurs: the lower front bone (pubis) points forwards, not back alongside the ischium (lower rear bone) as in ornithischians. The pelvis was immensely strong and contacted five vertebrae which were fused together for extra strength. This area of the animal had to bear enormous forces.

Apatosaurus Vertebrae (right) The nearest column of vertebrae are all shown in front view, the middle column in side view, and the far column shows them in rear view. The top row shows a neck vertebra. It is rather squat in appearance, mainly because the neural spine is low and split in two. This probably formed a guide in which a ligament ran. The body of the vertebra is excavated, forming pleurocoels, to lighten its weight. The middle row shows a back vertebra. This is less massive and has a higher neural spine which bears a prominent ridge for muscle attachments. The bottom row shows a tail vertebra. This is more lightly built but still provides plenty of attachment area for the tail muscles. These were probably used for swinging the whip-lash end of the tail.

Diplodocus Skull (left) Here the features of the diplodocids are seen clearly. In side view (top drawing) note the large eye-socket and fine pencil-like teeth at the front of the snout. In top view (lower drawing) you can see the unusual position of the nostrils.

Diplodocus Hand (below) The hand is broad and rather short as expected in such a massive animal. It is possible that only the first finger bore a large curved claw, and that the other fingers were finished off with a blunt pad, probably of horn.

Diplodocus Foot (below) Like the hand, the foot is short and broad with five rather stubby toes. Although the foot is often drawn with three clawed toes, at least one well-preserved specimen of *Diplodocus carnegiei* shows that only toes 1 and 2 bore claws.

Apatosaurus Skeleton (below) This is a much sturdier skeleton that that of *Diplodocus*. In particular note how much thicker the neck vertebrae are. The tail is especially long, containing perhaps 80 vertebrae and ending in a narrow whip-lash.

The prosauropods of the early Jurassic Period were replaced in the late Jurassic by some of the most amazingly large plant eating dinosaurs — indeed any animals — of all time. This second group of sauropodomorph dinosaurs are often called sauropods and include some of the most famous of all dinosaurs. The diplodocids are one group of sauropods that are very well known and include such types as *Diplodocus* (which gave its name to this particular group of sauropods), as well as *Apatosaurus* (also known by some as *Brontosaurus*) and some less well known forms such as *Dicraeosaurus, Nemegtosaurus* and *Antarctosaurus*.

Diplodocus (double beam) comes from Colorado, Wyoming and Utah. First discovered in the 1870s from remains that included parts of the back leg and many tail bones, it was not really until many years later that the animal was known well enough for its whole body to be reconstructed. Incidentally, the peculiar name 'double beam' comes from the fact that the tail bones in the fossils that were first discovered had rather strange pairs of bones on their underside (see the drawing on page 23).

Measuring almost 27m (90ft) in length and weighing in at something like 15 tonnes, this was a gigantic dinosaur although, as we shall see shortly, it was not the largest of all. *Diplodocus* had an enormously long neck and tail and stuck between them a very large body, with huge, long, pillar-like legs which supported the massive rib cage and belly.

The feet of the *Diplodocus* are round in outline like those of an elephant. They do not have the long toes of normal animals. They do, however, have one very large sharp claw on the inside edge of each front foot (see the *Diplodocus* hand above). This large claw may well have been used as a weapon of defence against large theropod meat eaters such as *Allosaurus* (pages 12-13) which lived at the same time as *Diplodocus*. Unlikely though it may seem, these dinosaurs were able to rear up on their back legs, like a bear is able to do, and slash out with their front legs in self-defence. I think it certain that young *Diplodocus*, the most likely prey of meat eaters such as *Allosaurus*, would have found this tactic very useful. Another defensive weapon that *Diplodocus* would have been able to use was the long tail. The end of the tail is extended into a long, thin whip-lash, which could have been flicked at attackers.

Diplodocus would have needed various sorts of defence because its head was far too small to have been any use at all. Although quite large by our standards (the head of a large *Diplodocus* is about 50-60cm (2ft) long), in comparison to the body the head is ridiculously small. The teeth are very unusual in that they are long and thin, like pencils and are found only at the front of the mouth. The head is quite sloping, and the nostrils are found up on the top of the head between the eyes (see above).

How could an animal that was so large manage to eat enough food to keep itself going? The answer would seem to be quite simple. Even though the head was small, the teeth are designed to be used like a rake. The long neck of these animals acted like the jib of a crane to lift the head high into the tree-tops (like a giraffe) so that it could take in lots of leaves and twigs, which would then be swallowed and stored in the huge stomach where all the goodness would have been slowly released.

Apatosaurus, Dicraeosaurus, Antarcotosaurus and *Nemegtosaurus* are all very similar to *Diplodocus* in body shape, although their heads vary a bit.

Camarasaurids & Brachiosaurids
Brachiosaurus (left) and Camarasaurus

These two groups of dinosaurs seem to be quite similar in many respects of their anatomy, but their outward appearance is noticeably different (see illustrations above and below). Both of these groups of dinosaurs are sauropods.

Camarasaurus from the western USA (Colorado, Wyoming and Utah) is the best example of Camarasaurids. *Camarasaurus* literally means 'chambered reptile', a name which refers to the holes that can be found in the sides of its backbone. You can see these on the illustrations of *Brachiosaurus* below, but similar ones can be seen in *Camarasaurus* (in fact they are also seen in almost all other sauropods). When the first remains of *Camarasaurus* were discovered it was thought that this feature was unique. It was soon discovered that this was not the case, but the name was not abandoned.

Much of the early material of *Camarasaurus* was very poorly preserved and it was not until 1924 that a reasonable specimen of this dinosaur was discovered. The dinosaur skeleton of 1924 was a beautifully preserved young *Camarasaurus*, which was about 6m (18ft) long. From odd leg bones and other fragments, we know that fully grown animals would have been 18m (60ft) long.

Compared to diplodocids, *Camarasaurus* had a shorter neck and tail without the whip-lash end, and had similar legs and chest. The main difference, however, is to be found in the head. The head of *Camarasaurus* is altogether chunkier and stronger looking than that of the diplodocids. It is much taller at the front and there are huge nostrils in front of the eyes. The teeth are also very different; they are large and appear spoon-shaped rather than pencil-shaped and are found along the sides of the mouth as well as at the front. *Camarasaurus* was therefore much shorter and more sturdy than diplodocids, lacking the whip-lash tail, but it had the slashing claw on its front feet. The shape of its teeth indicate that it did not use them to rake off leaves and twigs, but was able to bite off plant food between its sharp teeth before swallowing it.

Brachiosaurus (arm reptile) comes from North America and Africa and is found on rocks of the late Jurassic age. By far the best example of this dinosaur comes from Africa. An almost complete skeleton was found in rocks on Tendagura in Tanzania and was excavated between 1908 and 1912 by scientists from Germany. The whole dinosaur was shipped back to Berlin and erected in their Natural History Museum, where it stands to this day. The dinosaur is quite colossal. It stands some 23m (75ft) long (not as long as *Diplodocus*) but towers over it because its head stands some 12m (39ft) above the ground. It has been estimated by some scientists that this dinosaur may have weighed 70-80 tonnes.

The name of this dinosaur is not too hard to understand. The peculiar feature of *Brachiosaurus* is that its front legs (arms) are very much longer than is normal for dinosaurs. This gives them a very giraffe-like appearance, and they may well have used their enormous height advantage to feed from high branches.

In recent years several new brachiosaurids have been discovered in Colorada by a man called Jim Jensen; two of which (**Supersaurus** and **Ultrasaurus**) seem to have been even larger than *Brachiosaurus*.

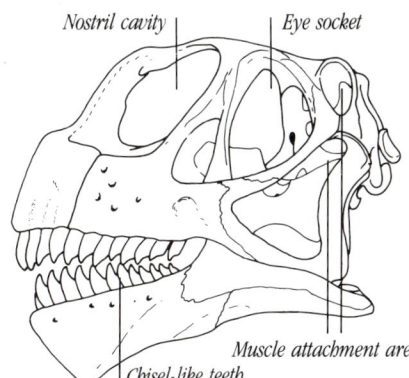

Camarasaurus Skull (above)
The skull of *Camarasaurus* is compact compared with that of diplodocids. The jaws are stout and support a closely packed array of chisel-like teeth. Above the level of the jaws the skull is high and spaciously designed. The large opening at the front of the skull is for extremely large nostrils. Immediately behind the nostril is the eye socket.

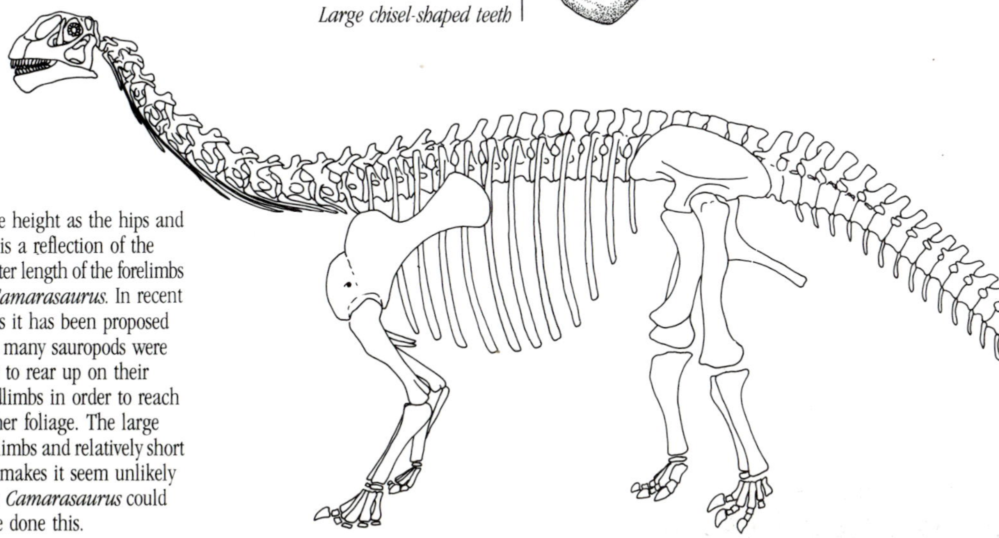

Camarasaurus Skeleton (right)
The skeletal reconstruction seen here is based on the work of Charles Gilmore. The proportions of the skeleton are notably different from the diplodocids. The skull is relatively large and deep, and is supported on a short neck which was evidently quite flexible. The ribs of the neck are long and slender and no doubt provided for the attachment of large muscles. The short neck means that the range of plants available to *Camarasaurus* must have been limited to the lower branches of trees and plants closer to ground level. As reconstructed here the shoulder region is at the same height as the hips and this is a reflection of the greater length of the forelimbs of *Camarasaurus*. In recent years it has been proposed that many sauropods were able to rear up on their hindlimbs in order to reach higher foliage. The large forelimbs and relatively short tail makes it seem unlikely that *Camarasaurus* could have done this.

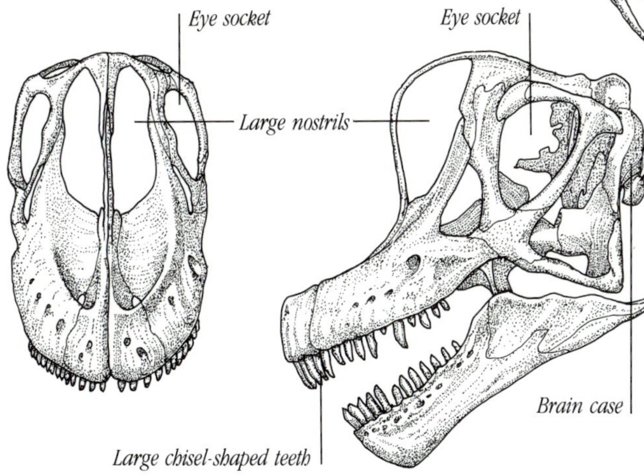

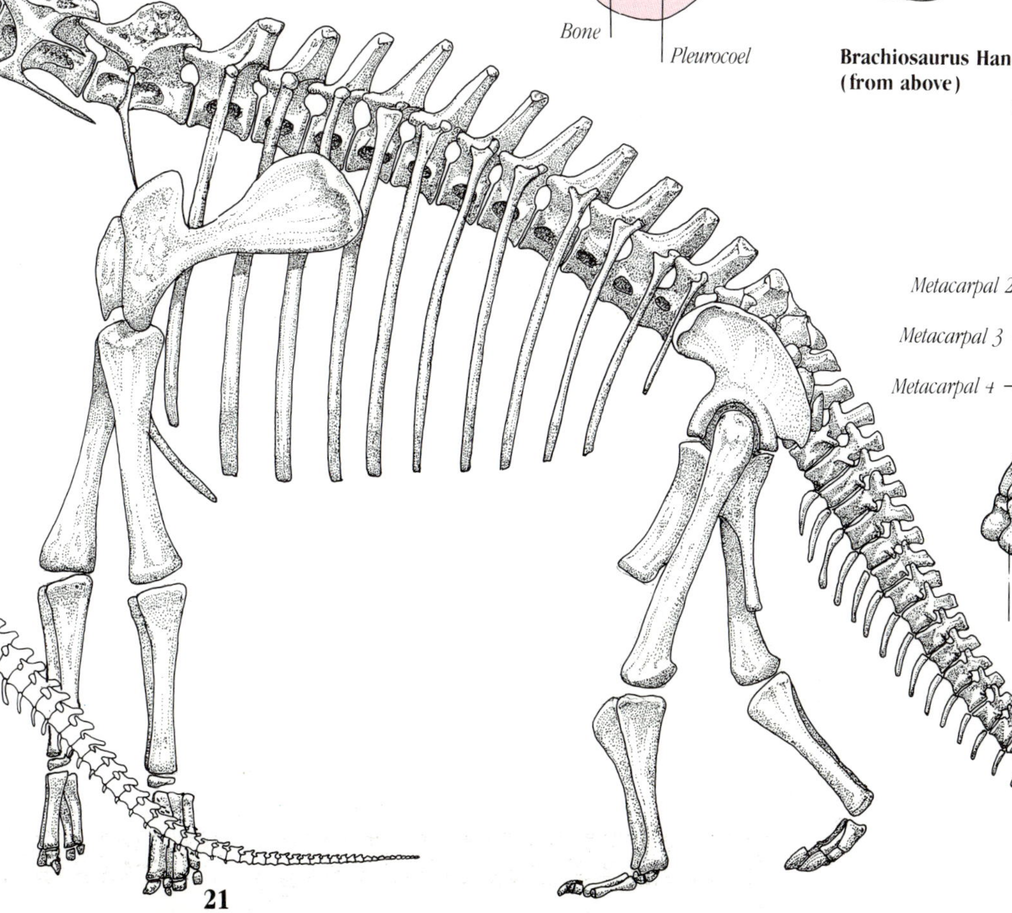

Brachiosaurus Skeleton (right)
This reconstruction of *Brachiosaurus* was made by Werner Janensch from the material collected at Tendaguru (1908-1912). A complete skeleton is mounted in the Museum of Natural History, Berlin. The similarity to a giraffe is quite striking with the long front legs lifting the shoulders above the hips and the neck raising the head to over 13m (42ft) in the original specimen. The spines on the neck are heavily scarred for the attachment of muscles to raise and hold the neck in position. The rib cage is quite narrow and deep, as in an elephant, and the feet are similarly narrow and compact. Unlike most sauropods, the tail is relatively short.

Brachiosaurus Skull (right)
In profile, this skull shows certain similarities to that of *Camarasaurus*. The jaws are stout and support large chisel-shaped teeth. The signs of heavy wear on these teeth suggest that these animals preferred abrasive plants. The unusual size of the nostrils may indicate either a powerful sense of smell, a resonating device or a cooling surface for the blood.

Brachiosaurus Rib

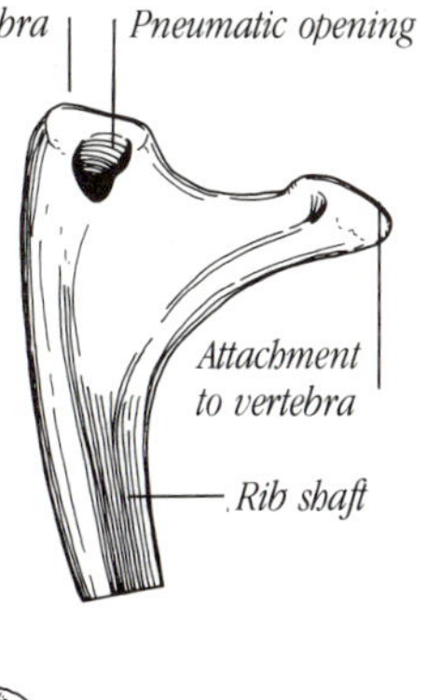

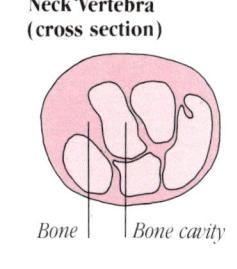

Brachiosaurus Rib (left) and Sectioned Vertebrae (right)
Brachiosaurus has many weight-saving features. The ribs in the chest region have a pneumatic opening near the top which leads to an air passage down the shaft of the rib. The cross section through a neck vertebra (top right) reveals the remarkable system of air spaces, while that of the back vertebra shows the extensive pleurocoels separated by a very thin sheet of bone (bony areas shown in red). The vertebra closely resembles an I-section girder.

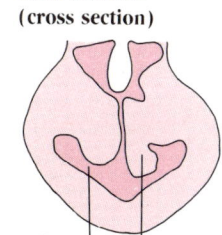

Neck Vertebra (cross section)

Back Vertebra (cross section)

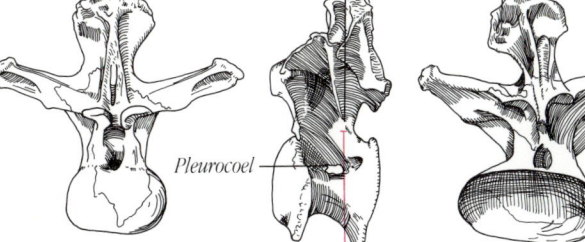

Neck Vertebra

Back Vertebra

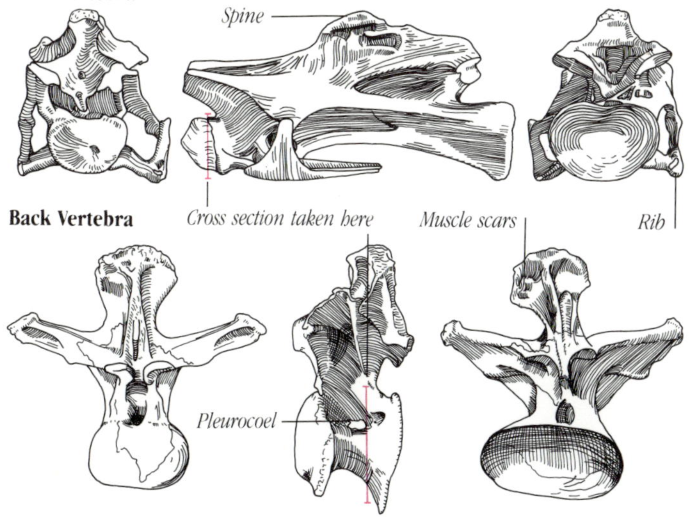

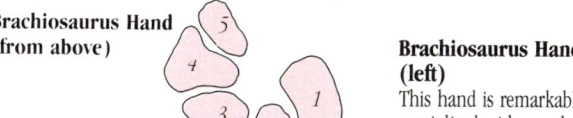

Brachiosaurus Vertebrae (left)
The neck vertebrae are long, narrow, elongated structures with a low spine on which muscles attached. The front end of the neck vertebra has a rounded surface that forms a strong and flexible joint against the cup-shaped depression on the rear of the vertebra in front of it. The back vertebrae are taller and squatter to withstand supporting the weight of this animal. The tall spine is scarred for the attachment of muscles; the large 'wings' projecting from its foot support the ends of the ribs. The red lines show where the cross sections are taken.

Brachiosaurus Hand (from above)

Brachiosaurus Hand (left)
This hand is remarkably specialised with very long metacarpals which are clustered closely together as can be seen in the top drawing. The toes (so far as they are known) have just one small bone on the end of each metacarpal except for the 1st toe which bears a small claw.

Camarasaurus Foot (below)
Camarasaurus' right foot has five short toes which are widely splayed to form a broad weight-bearing arrangement. The inner toe is larger and possesses a narrow curved claw which may have been used for self-defence. The foot of *Brachiosaurus* is only known from isolated bones.

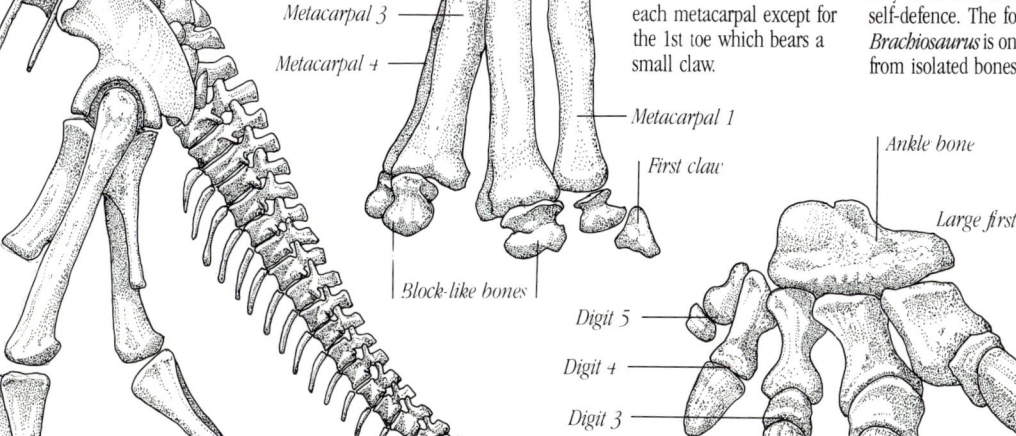

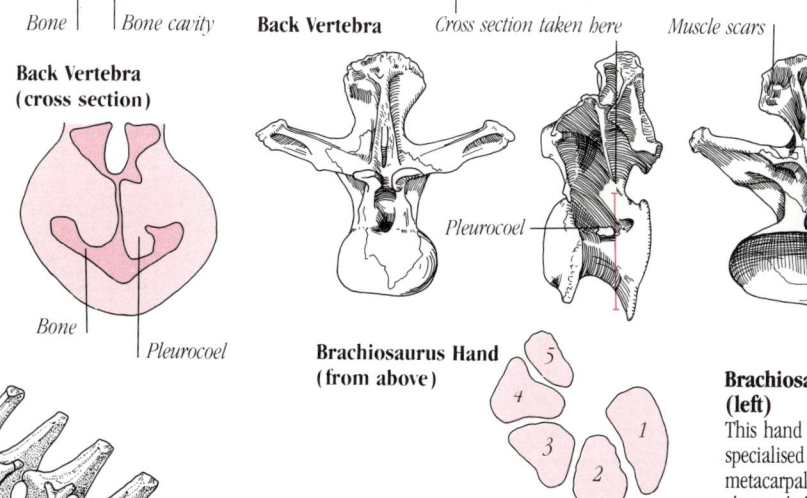

Miscellaneous Sauropods

From left to right: Vulcanodon, Saltasaurus, Opisthocoelicaudia

Sauropod Armour (below)

Recent work in Argentina has resulted in the discovery that some sauropods had bony armour plating. The first plates to be described are those of *Saltasaurus* and *Laplatasaurus*, and some are shown below. One type of plate with a low mid-line ridge has been referred to *Laplatasaurus*; the others are regarded as typical of *Saltasaurus*. These are variable in size and shape ranging from large, ridged plates (below middle) to the sheets of densely-packed, tiny nodular bones illustrated below right.

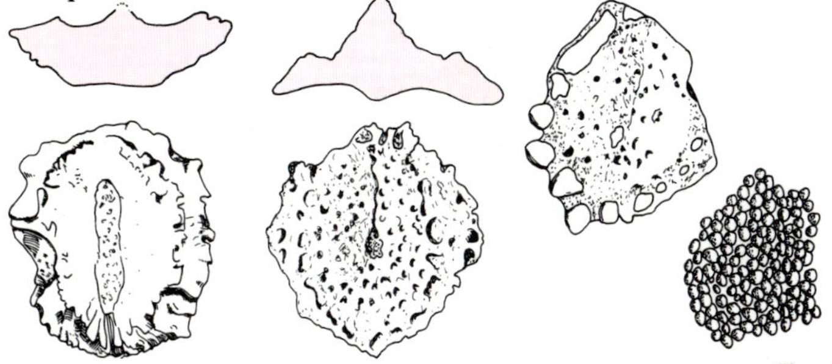

Laplatasaurus

Saltasaurus

Omeisaurus Skull (right)

This skull is unusual when compared with those of other sauropods. It is wedge-shaped in side view and has typically sauropod struts of bone dividing large skull spaces. However, the nostrils are much nearer the front of the snout than in other sauropods. Though appearing to be toothless, there are sockets for at least 32 teeth in the upper jaw and 28-34 in the lower. The drawing is based on one included in Dong Zhiming's 1983 review of dinosaurs of south-central China.

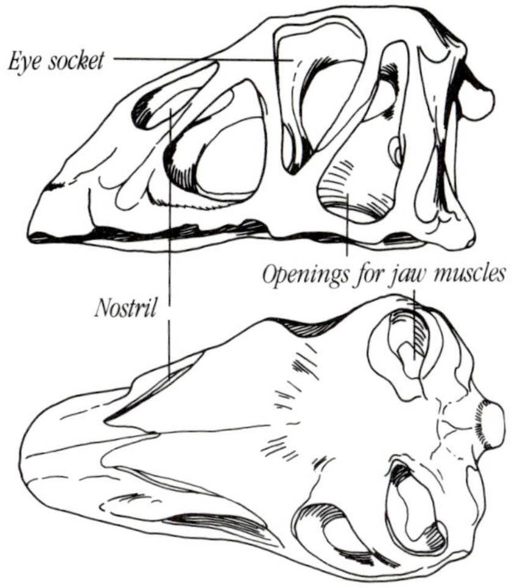

Eye socket
Nostril
Openings for jaw muscles

Opisthocoelicaudia Skeleton (below)

This reconstruction is based on the work of Magdalena Borsuk-Bialynicka. This dinosaur is currently only known from its headless skeleton so its relationships with other sauropods are not precisely known. It has an extremely unusual tail: the ball-and-socket joint between vertebrae works by means of a socket in the *rear* of each vertebra—unlike any other sauropod. As a result the joints between vertebrae are remarkably strong. Note the massive pelvic region.

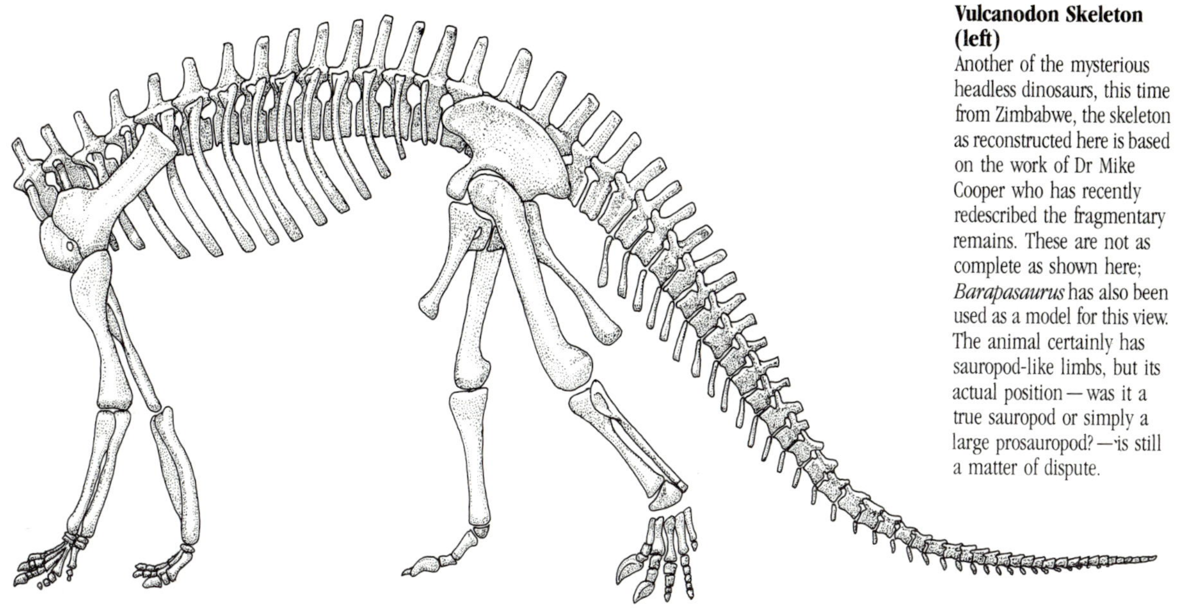

Vulcanodon Skeleton (left)

Another of the mysterious headless dinosaurs, this time from Zimbabwe, the skeleton as reconstructed here is based on the work of Dr Mike Cooper who has recently redescribed the fragmentary remains. These are not as complete as shown here; *Barapasaurus* has also been used as a model for this view. The animal certainly has sauropod-like limbs, but its actual position — was it a true sauropod or simply a large prosauropod? — is still a matter of dispute.

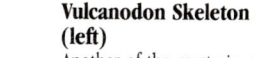

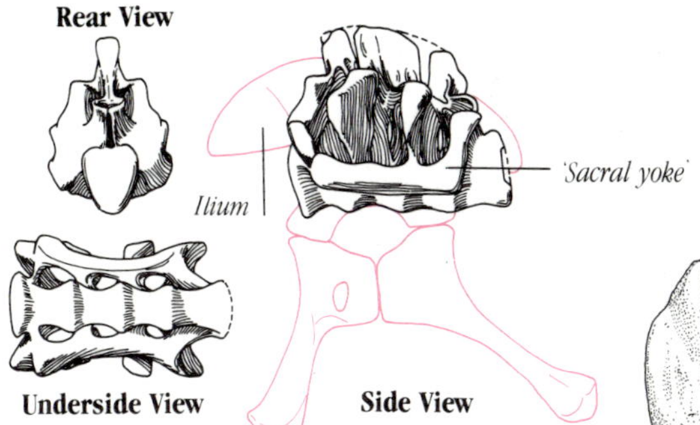

Rear View
Ilium
'Sacral yoke'
Underside View
Side View

Barapasaurus Sacrum and Pelvis (above)

There are four vertebrae in the sacrum, all firmly fused together. On either side, the ribs are short, stout and welded together to form a sacral yoke. This attached firmly to the inner surface of the ilium.

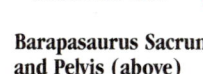
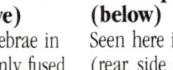
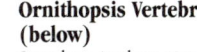

Ornithopsis Vertebra (below)

Seen here in three views (rear, side and front), this vertebra is very similar to that of *Brachiosaurus*, and may indicate a relationship. The large weight-saving pleurocoels are particularly noticeable.

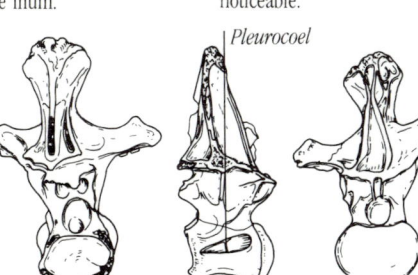
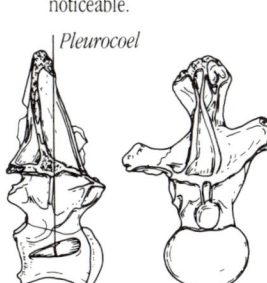
Pleurocoel

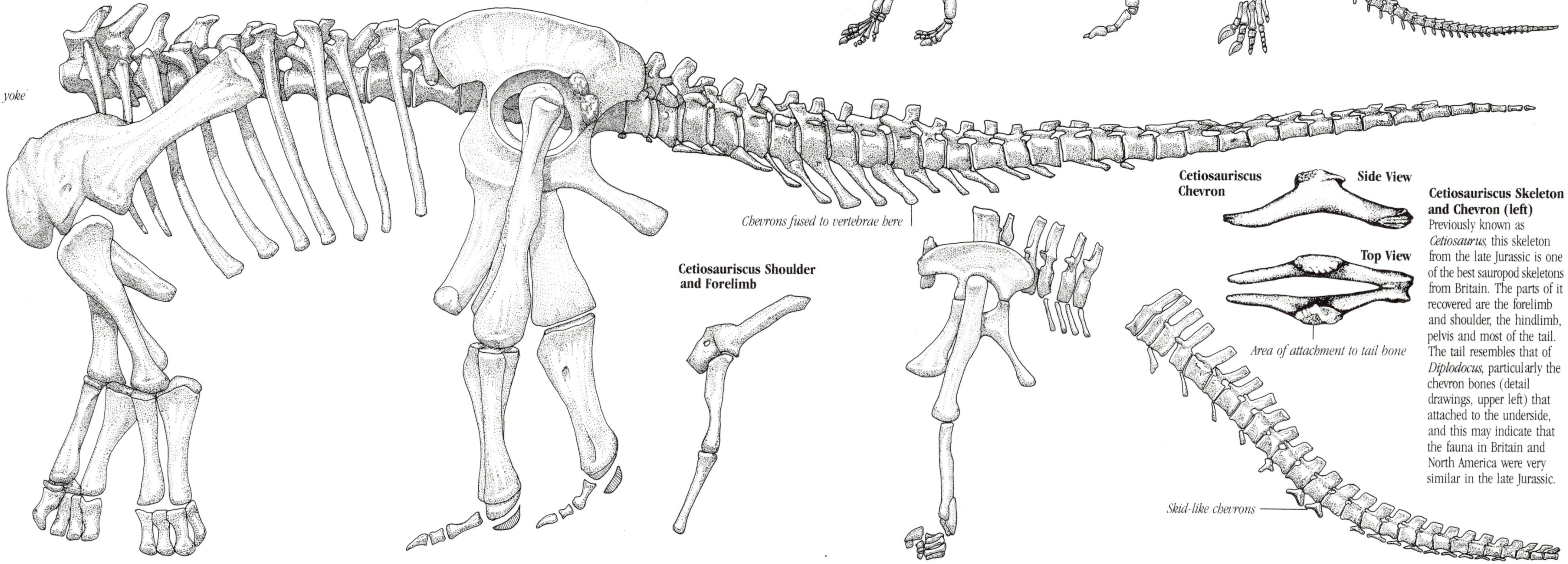

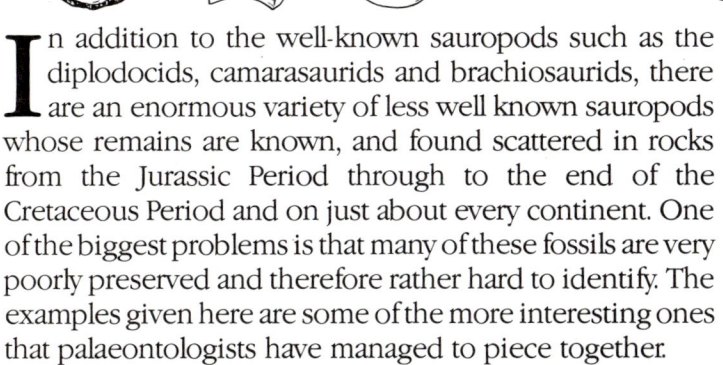

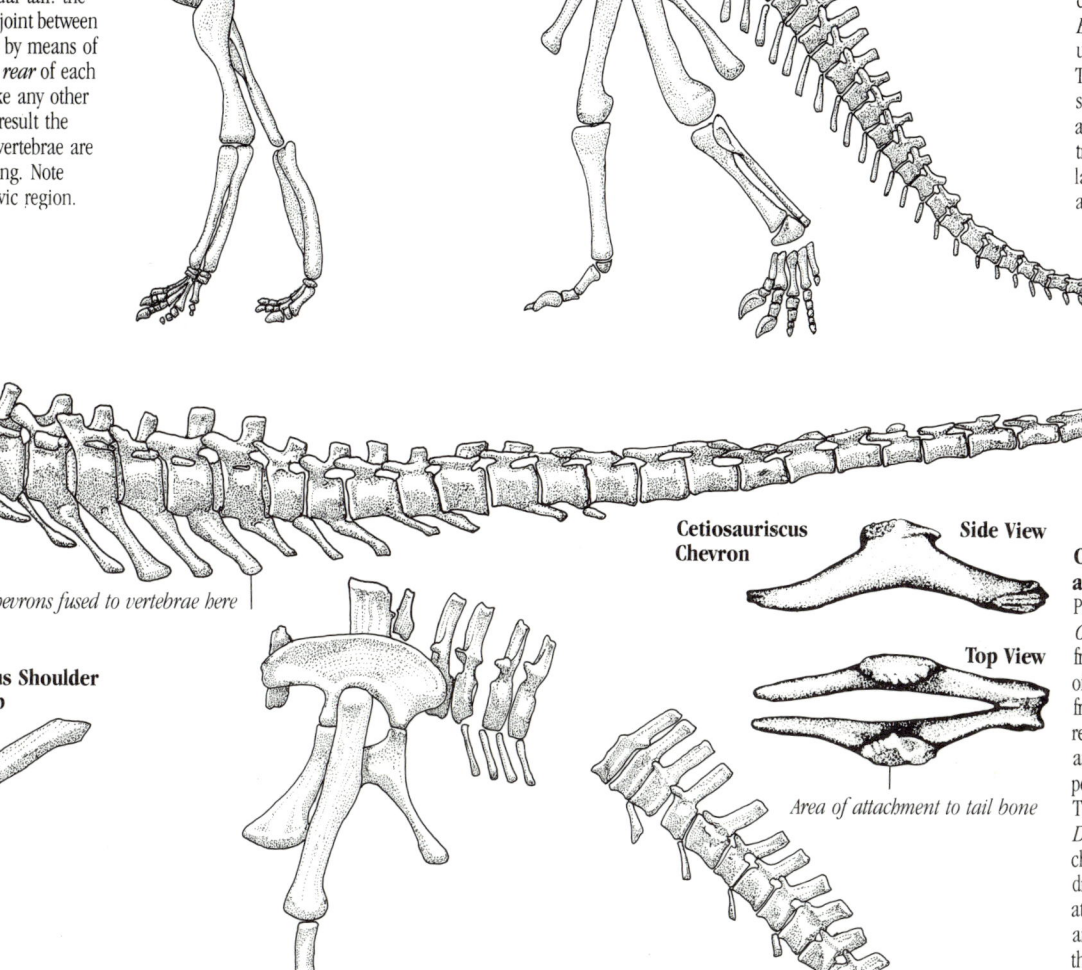

Chevrons fused to vertebrae here

Cetiosauriscus Shoulder and Forelimb

Cetiosauriscus Chevron
Side View
Top View
Area of attachment to tail bone
Skid-like chevrons

Cetiosauriscus Skeleton and Chevron (left)

Previously known as *Cetiosaurus*, this skeleton from the late Jurassic is one of the best sauropod skeletons from Britain. The parts of it recovered are the forelimb and shoulder, the hindlimb, pelvis and most of the tail. The tail resembles that of *Diplodocus*, particularly the chevron bones (detail drawings, upper left) that attached to the underside, and this may indicate that the fauna in Britain and North America were very similar in the late Jurassic.

In addition to the well-known sauropods such as the diplodocids, camarasaurids and brachiosaurids, there are an enormous variety of less well known sauropods whose remains are known, and found scattered in rocks from the Jurassic Period through to the end of the Cretaceous Period and on just about every continent. One of the biggest problems is that many of these fossils are very poorly preserved and therefore rather hard to identify. The examples given here are some of the more interesting ones that palaeontologists have managed to piece together.

Vulcanodon (fire tooth) is one of the earliest known sauropods. Its remains come from early Jurassic rocks in Zimbabwe and consist of part of the rear end of a large, 6m (20ft) long, dinosaur. As indicated above, we are not even sure precisely what the rear of the animal looked like since we have had to use the remains of another early dinosaur *Barapasaurus* (from India) for part of this reconstruction. According to some this is one of the first sauropods known, and it is therefore very interesting scientifically, but it would obviously be much better if more of the skeleton was preserved.

Saltasaurus (reptile from Salta Province, Argentina) is another extraordinary sauropod, which this time comes from South America. First reported by José Bonaparte and Jaime Powell in 1980, the fossil remains of *Saltasaurus* are from rocks of late Cretaceous age and, although they are far from complete, provide the most unexpected evidence on the appearance of at least some sauropods. While much of the skeleton has the shape typical of most sauropods, also found among the remains are large, knobbly plates and smaller pieces of bone of a type that had been thought only to belong to the armoured ornithischian dinosaurs (see pages 44-47). This is a most unexpected discovery and indicates that some, at least, were able to defend themselves against attack from theropods by using armour-plating instead of by fighting back. *Saltasaurus* seems to have reached a length of about 12m (40ft).

Opisthocoelicaudia (posterior cavity tail) is yet another unusual sauropod from the late Cretaceous Period. This time it comes from Mongolia, where it was discovered in 1965. As was the case with *Vulcanodon*, the skeleton of this creature lacks the head and neck. The skeleton was of an animal some 12m (40ft) in length and quite heavily built, with powerful legs and thick ribs. The unusual feature of this dinosaur was that it had a very short tail (by sauropod standards) which could be used as a prop. It enabled these animals to rear up into trees to reach the higher and more tender leaves while using the tail to sit back on in order to keep their balance. Peculiar joints in the tail helped them to use the tail in this way, which is the reason for the strange scientific name of this dinosaur. Again, it is very frustrating not to know what the head of this dinosaur looked like because the head and teeth would enable us to distinguish which group of sauropods they belong to.

Heads of these dinosaurs are so often missing from the skeletons that there may be more than just coincidence in it. It seems quite likely that the head and neck were either the first things to be eaten by scavenging dinosaurs, or they were the first things to rot away from the carcass of the dead animal after it had died and before it was buried in mud. Some fossilised bones have shown evidence of gnawing.

Omeisaurus from China is unusually preserved as just a head and part of a neck, while ***Ornithopsis*** and ***Cetiosauriscus*** are rather fragmentary forms found in Britain.

FABROSAURIDS & HETERODONTOSAURIDS
From left to right: Scutellosaurus, Lesothosaurus, Heterodontosaurus

Heterodontosaurus Skeleton (right)
The reconstructed skeleton of *Heterodontosaurus* shows it to be a lightly-built, agile animal, typical of the early ornithopods. In particular notice how the foot bones (metatarsals) and lower leg bones are elongated relative to the upper leg bone (femur). This kind of long, slender hind leg is a sure sign of a fleet-footed runner which presumably relied on speed to escape from its predators. The long, tapering tail acted as a counterbalance for the front half of the body and was probably held out almost horizontally above the ground when the animal ran. The front limbs are very robust compared with those of *Lesothosaurus* and in particular the fingers and wrist bones are well-developed. Also visible are the bony rods lying along the backbone, which are characteristic of bipedal ornithischians; they were present in order to stiffen the back, hips and tail.

Lesothosaurus Skeleton (right)
This animal is another typical early ornithopod but it does not show the specialisations of a robust front leg and fused lower hind leg bones seen in *Heterodontosaurus*. In that form the front leg may have been used for digging or in defending itself or possibly even in tearing down vegetation. In both forms the neck is long and flexible, perhaps useful for getting the head into vegetation to pick off shoots or buds, or for keeping an eye out for predators.

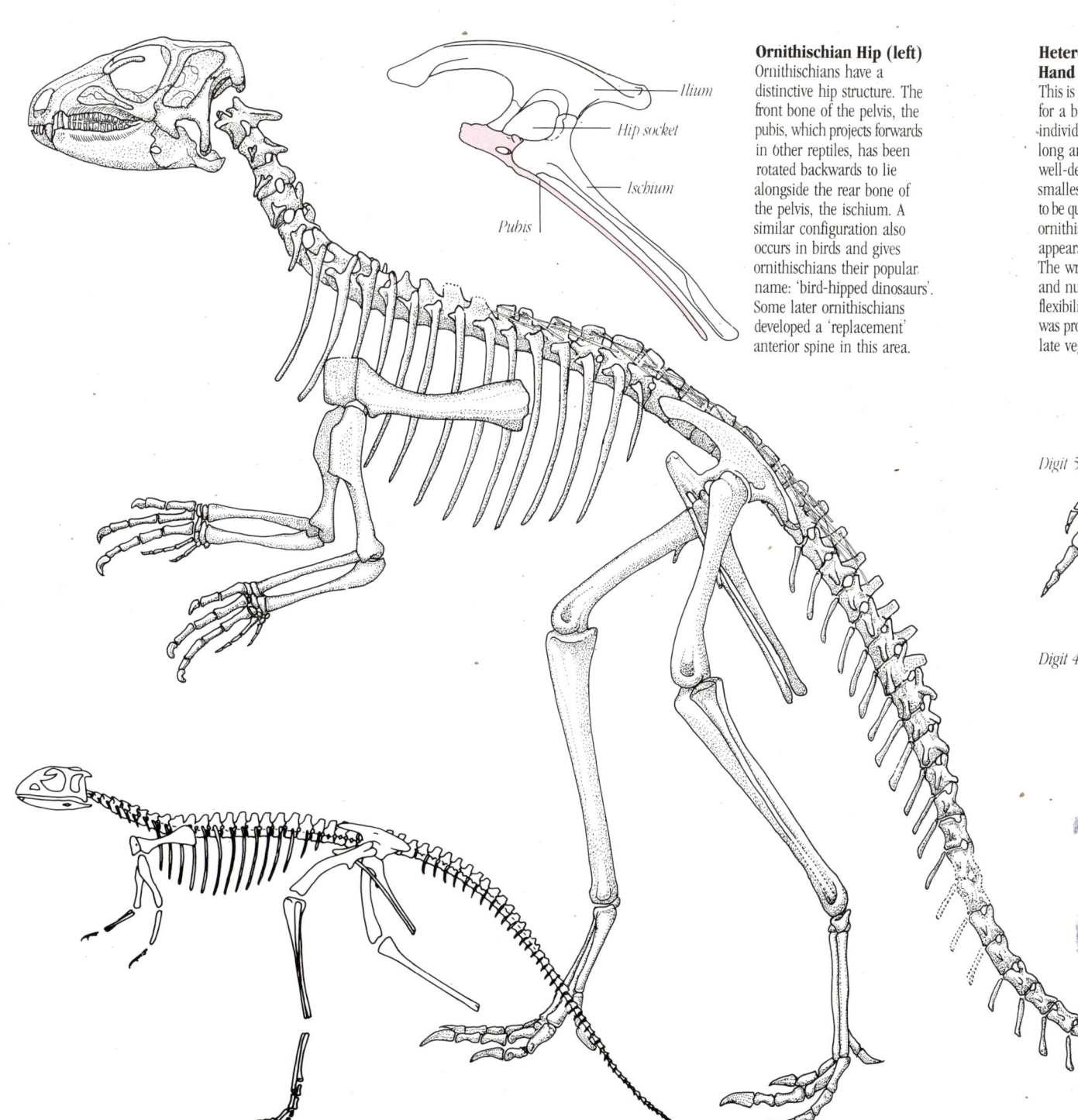

Ornithischian Hip (left)
Ornithischians have a distinctive hip structure. The front bone of the pelvis, the pubis, which projects forwards in other reptiles, has been rotated backwards to lie alongside the rear bone of the pelvis, the ischium. A similar configuration also occurs in birds and gives ornithischians their popular name: 'bird-hipped dinosaurs'. Some later ornithischians developed a 'replacement' anterior spine in this area.

Heterodontosaurus Hand (below)
This is particularly well-made for a bipedal dinosaur. The individual finger bones are long and slender, and bear well-developed claws. The smallest finger does not seem to be quite so off-set as in some ornithischians, so the hand appears more symmetrical. The wrist bones are small and numerous, suggesting flexibility. *Heterodontosaurus* was probably able to manipulate vegetation quite adeptly.

Heterodontosaurus Foot (below right)
The foot bones are long and slender, reflecting that the animal possessing them was both a runner, and small and light — the foot did not have to be specially strengthened to bear the animal's weight. Notice how the smallest toe is reversed relative to the others. This may have given the foot extra surface area for bearing the animal's weight. The metatarsal bones are particularly elongated.

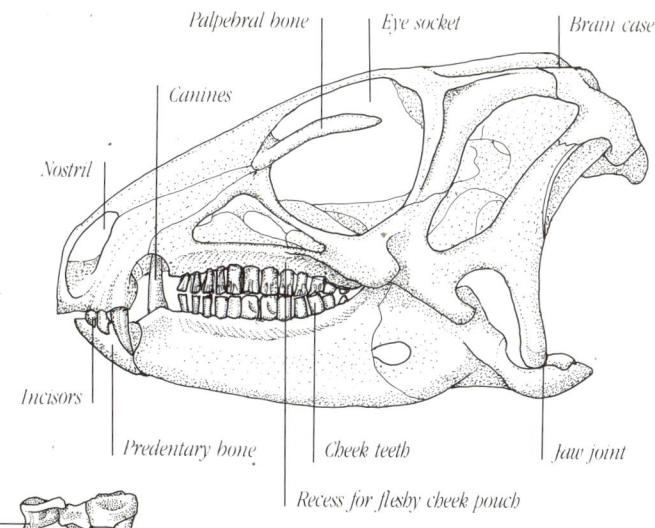

Heterodontosaurus Skull (left)
In this form the teeth may have chewed up food, rather than simply cropping it. There are various theories about how the chewing action was produced: it might have been caused by back and forwards movement of the lower jaw, but perhaps more likely, the lower jaw might have rotated relative to the upper jaw as it closed. The large tusks are probably a male characteristic.

Lesothosaurus Skull (left)
The cheek teeth here are much more slender and leaf-like, used perhaps for shredding food, but not chewing it. This form may have had a salt-gland and if so this could indicate that the animal lived in an arid environment, needing to conserve its body water. Doing this leads to a build-up of body salts which must be disposed of by the salt-gland. Note how the small teeth are separated.

Tuskless Heterodontosaurus Skull (left)
The lack of tusks in this specimen may indicate that it is a female of a tusked *Heterodontosaurus* since in other respects it is almost identical (compare with skull shown at top left). If this is so then it shows that even if the tusks were used in feeding, they were also used as a sexual signal — distinguishing males from females. The muscles shown on the skull are responsible for closing the jaw and also for producing the forces which cause the chewing action of the jaw.

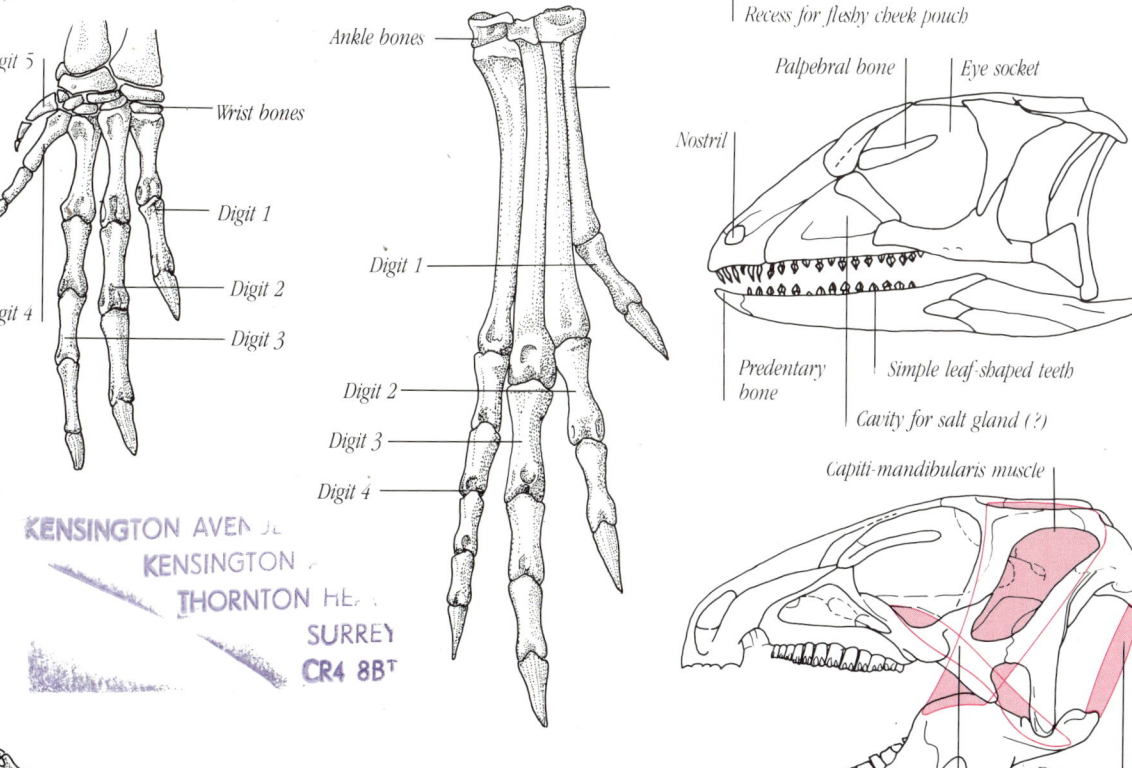

As described in the Introduction, ornithischian dinosaurs are all plant eaters, and have several other features that are not seen in saurischian dinosaurs. They have a bird-like arrangement of hip bones (from which they get their unusual name), a horn-covered beak at the tip of the jaw and thin bony rods along the sides of the backbone.

As was the case with the saurischian dinosaurs, there are a number of different types of ornithischian: ornithopods, ceratopians, pachycephalosaurs, stegosaurs and ankylosaurs (see 'Dinosaur Family Tree' page 5). The first group we shall be looking at are the ornithopods — a group of quite abundant dinosaurs which are found throughout the reign of the dinosaurs.

Fabrosaurids are a group of small — about 1m (3ft) long — dinosaurs that ran mainly on their back legs, of which *Lesothosaurus* and *Scutellosaurus* are examples (see above). In general shape they look rather like small theropods. The back legs are long and powerful, enabling these animals to run very fast, and the body was balanced over the hips by a long muscular tail. The arms and hands are not as strong as they are in the small theropods, and do not have the extremely sharp talons that are found on the hands of the meat eaters.

What we have in the case of these small ornithopods is the plant eating equivalent of the coelurosaurs; animals that can run extremely fast to avoid getting caught by predators.

The diet of plants of these animals is indicated by their teeth, in just the same way as in the prosauropods (pages 16-17). The teeth are small and not dagger-like as in meat eaters, but leaf-shaped, with rough edges that are ideal for shredding leaves and twigs. Unlike prosauropods, these dinosaurs also have the horny beak at the front of the mouth, with is ideal for nipping off shoots and buds.

Lesothosaurus (reptile from Lesotho) is known from southern Africa. Its remains have been found in rocks that are from the early Jurassic Period.

Scutellosaurus (bony-plate dinosaur) comes from Arizona, and is also of early Jurassic age. Discovered more recently, this animal is really quite similar to *Lesothosaurus*. except for the fact that is seems to have had lots of small, protective bony studs in the skin of its back. These would have been like the bony studs in the skin of crocodiles, and would have protected it against meat-eating dinosaurs. It seems quite possible that *Scutellosaurus* is an ancestor of the later, very heavily armoured ankylosaurs (pages 44-47).

Heterodontosaurids were another early group of ornithopod dinosaurs. Most heterodontosaurids are known from southern Africa, but more recently there are reports of these dinosaurs from North America. Like the two fabrosaurids described above, they lived during the early part of the Jurassic, but while a few fabrosaurs are known from later times, no heterodontosaurids seem to have survived beyond this age.

Heterodontosaurus (mixed-tooth reptile) is the best known of these dinosaurs because a complete skeleton has been found. It looks similar to *Lesothosaurus* in many ways, but there are some important differences. Its hands and arms are unusually large and have surprisingly sharp claws. The head is peculiar because there are large tusks near the front of the the mouth and the teeth are well built for slicing as well as shredding plants. It seems that *Heterodontosaurus* was a strong little dinosaur, well able to defend itself against the smaller meat eaters of the time.

HYPSILOPHODONTIDS
From top to bottom: Tenontosaurus, Dryosaurus, Hypsilophodon

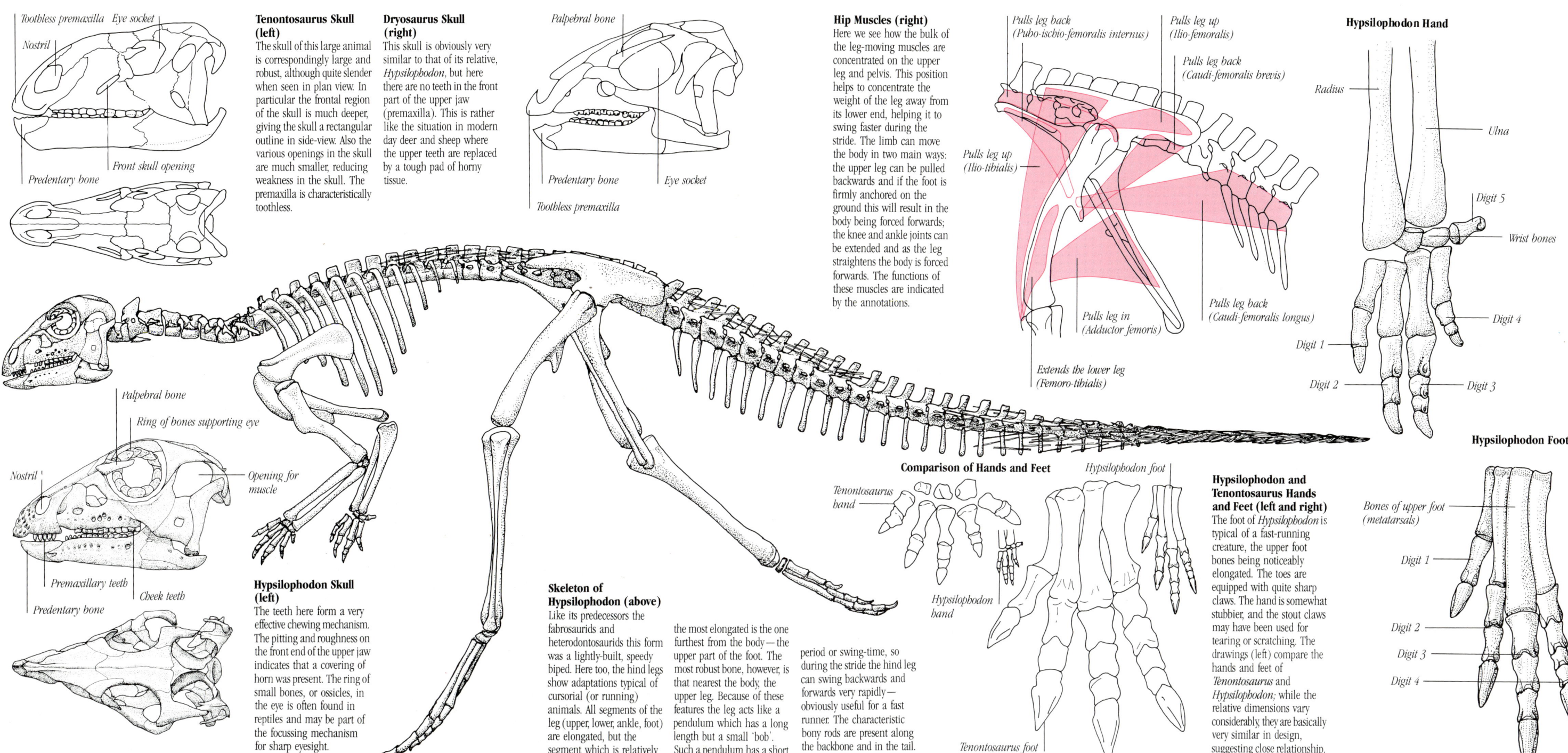

Tenontosaurus Skull (left)
The skull of this large animal is correspondingly large and robust, although quite slender when seen in plan view. In particular the frontal region of the skull is much deeper, giving the skull a rectangular outline in side-view. Also the various openings in the skull are much smaller, reducing weakness in the skull. The premaxilla is characteristically toothless.

Dryosaurus Skull (right)
This skull is obviously very similar to that of its relative, *Hypsilophodon*, but here there are no teeth in the front part of the upper jaw (premaxilla). This is rather like the situation in modern day deer and sheep where the upper teeth are replaced by a tough pad of horny tissue.

Hip Muscles (right)
Here we see how the bulk of the leg-moving muscles are concentrated on the upper leg and pelvis. This position helps to concentrate the weight of the leg away from its lower end, helping it to swing faster during the stride. The limb can move the body in two main ways: the upper leg can be pulled backwards and if the foot is firmly anchored on the ground this will result in the body being forced forwards; the knee and ankle joints can be extended and as the leg straightens the body is forced forwards. The functions of these muscles are indicated by the annotations.

Hypsilophodon Skull (left)
The teeth here form a very effective chewing mechanism. The pitting and roughness on the front end of the upper jaw indicates that a covering of horn was present. The ring of small bones, or ossicles, in the eye is often found in reptiles and may be part of the focussing mechanism for sharp eyesight.

Skeleton of Hypsilophodon (above)
Like its predecessors the fabrosaurids and heterodontosaurids this form was a lightly-built, speedy biped. Here too, the hind legs show adaptations typical of cursorial (or running) animals. All segments of the leg (upper, lower, ankle, foot) are elongated, but the segment which is relatively the most elongated is the one furthest from the body — the upper part of the foot. The most robust bone, however, is that nearest the body, the upper leg. Because of these features the leg acts like a pendulum which has a long length but a small 'bob'. Such a pendulum has a short period or swing-time, so during the stride the hind leg can swing backwards and forwards very rapidly — obviously useful for a fast runner. The characteristic bony rods are present along the backbone and in the tail.

Comparison of Hands and Feet

Hypsilophodon and Tenontosaurus Hands and Feet (left and right)
The foot of *Hypsilophodon* is typical of a fast-running creature, the upper foot bones being noticeably elongated. The toes are equipped with quite sharp claws. The hand is somewhat stubbier, and the stout claws may have been used for tearing or scratching. The drawings (left) compare the hands and feet of *Tenontosaurus* and *Hypsilophodon*; while the relative dimensions vary considerably, they are basically very similar in design, suggesting close relationship.

Hypsilophodontids are quite widespread dinosaurs that seem to have taken over from the fabrosaurids and heterodontosaurids after the middle of the Jurassic Period. Most hypsilophodontids are very similar to fabrosaurids in appearance. Illustrated above are three of the best examples.

Dryosaurus (wood reptile) is one of the earliest well preserved hypsilophodontids. Its fossilised remains were discovered in North America and also come from Africa and perhaps Europe as well. They were found in rocks of late Jurassic age; in fact their remains are found in the same rocks as the giant sauropod dinosaurs (pages 18-21). It is medium-sized compared with most other ornithopods, ranging from 3-4m (10-13ft). As in the previous types that we have looked at, the body is reasonably short and compact for a plant eater. The reason for this is that the hip bones of all ornithischians are arranged to allow the main part of the belly to hang between the legs rather than in front of the hips, as was the case in the sauropodomorphs (pages 16-23). This means that the tail does not have to be excessively long to balance the front part of the body over the hips. The head is fairly small, and the jaws end in a neat little horny beak that is ideal for nipping off shoots and buds as well as for slicing through foliage. The beak would have been very similar to the beak of a turtle.

Hypsilophodon (high-crested tooth) is another of these dinosaurs and is the one that gave its name to the group as a whole. It comes from southern Britain, where it is found in rocks of early Cretaceous age. Several skeletons of this small dinosaur were found toward the end of the last century, which allowed us to learn quite a lot about it. *Hypsilophodon* was comparatively small; most of the skeletons that are known are of animals that are no more than about 1.5m (4ft) long and the largest known specimen is something like 2.5m (6-7ft) long.

It differs from *Dryosaurus* in certain small ways, among the most noticeable of which are the teeth running along the sides of its beak and the extra toe that it has on its back foot. Another thing that *Hypsilophodon* shows very well are the thin, bony rods that lie alongside the backbone. These help to stiffen and strengthen the back when running. The strange thing about these bones in *Hypsilophodon* is that while most ornithischians have these along the middle of the back, *Hypsilophodon* also has many of them tightly packed around the end of its tail. At first these were a bit of a puzzle, but it is now thought that they were there for the same reason that they are found in the tails of meat eaters like the dromaeosaurids (pages 10-11); they stiffened the tail so that it could help them to balance and also to change direction quickly when running at speed. So, while the meat eaters evolved specially modified stiff tails to help them to catch prey on the run, some of the plant eaters that they preyed upon evolved exactly the same thing to escape!

Until quite recently, it was thought by many scientists that *Hypsilophodon* lived in trees, a bit like the tree-kangaroos that are found in Papua New Guinea. Unfortunately, this was completely incorrect as was pointed out by Peter Galton of Bridgeport University.

Tenontosaurus (stiff reptile) is the largest of the known hypsilophodontids and was found in the 1960s in Montana. It too comes from rocks of lower Cretaceous age. The name refers to its tail which was also stiffened by bony rods.

New discoveries have also unearthed hypsilophodontids in China and Australia.

IGUANODONTIDS
Clockwise from top right: Ouranosaurus, Iguanodon, Camptosaurus, Muttaburrasaurus

Skull Comparison (below)
The skulls of these iguanodontids show considerable differences, despite all being large compared to the body, having long snouts, and ending in a broad, toothless beak. The *Iguanodon* skull has a generalised structure but that of *Camptosaurus* is lower at the back and has a comparatively narrower snout. The skull of *Muttaburrasaurus* is the most peculiar, with a remarkable bump above and behind its nostrils. We do not know what this was for but it may have been implicated in sexual recognition. The Mongolian form, *Iguanodon orientalis*, has a similar protruberance. These three forms represent a wide distribution for iguanodontids, coming from Europe, North America and Australia respectively.

Jaw Muscles (below)
The jaw muscles of *Ouranosaurus* are large and powerful as expected in a large ornithopod. Muscle 1 arises from a large opening in the skull and it has a firm insertion on to a projection of the lower jaw (coronoid process). This insertion increases the moment arm of the muscle, a measure of the force which it can produce.

Ouranosaurus Skeleton

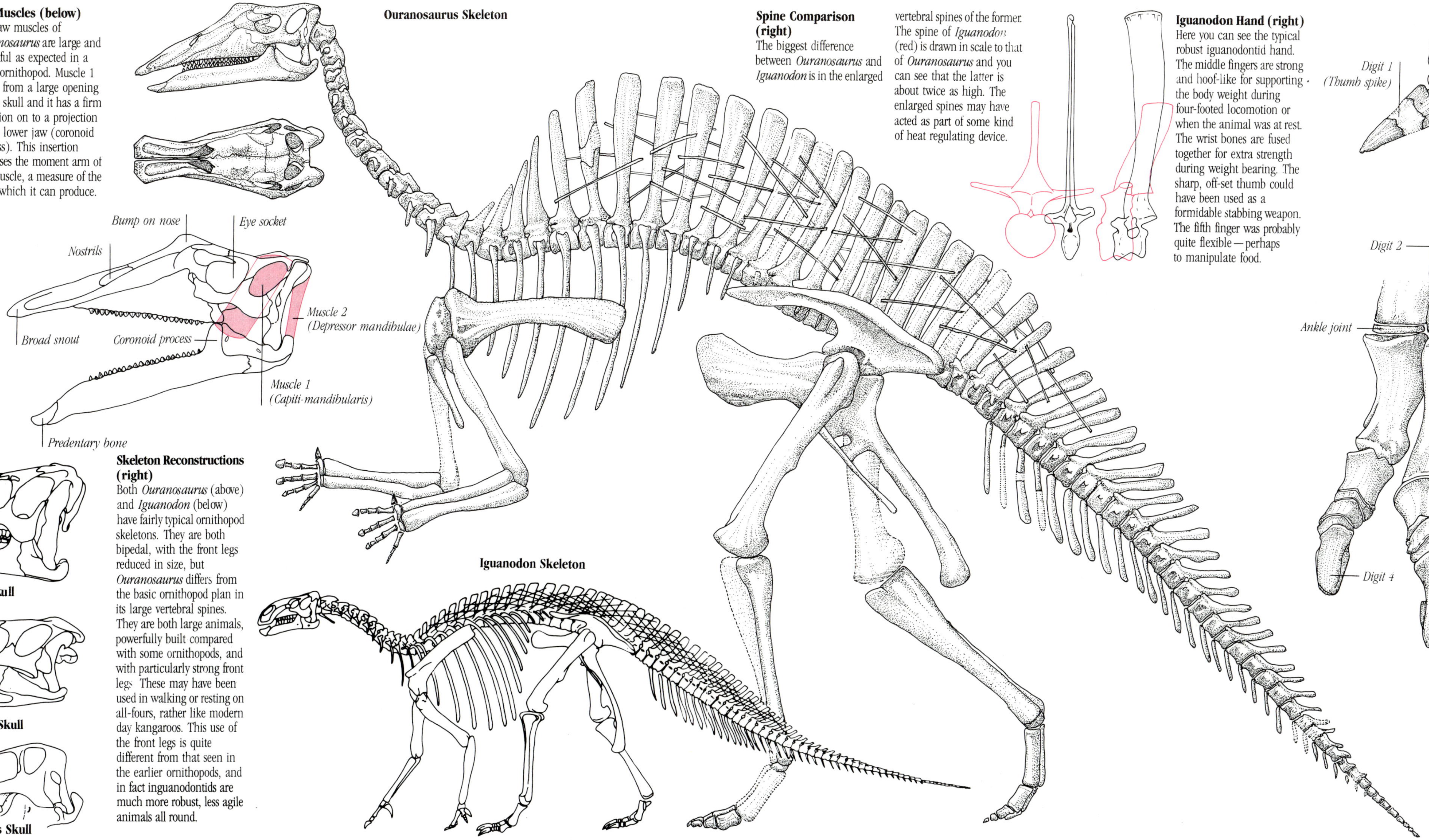

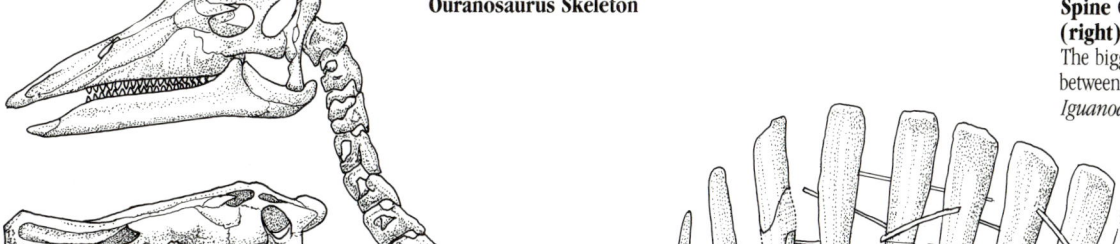

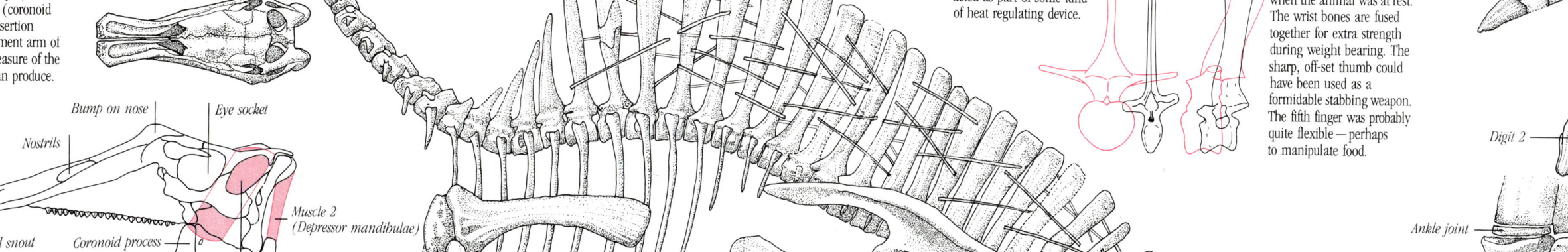

Spine Comparison (right)
The biggest difference between *Ouranosaurus* and *Iguanodon* is in the enlarged vertebral spines of the former. The spine of *Iguanodon* (red) is drawn in scale to that of *Ouranosaurus* and you can see that the latter is about twice as high. The enlarged spines may have acted as part of some kind of heat regulating device.

Iguanodon Hand (right)
Here you can see the typical robust iguanodontid hand. The middle fingers are strong and hoof-like for supporting the body weight during four-footed locomotion or when the animal was at rest. The wrist bones are fused together for extra strength during weight bearing. The sharp, off-set thumb could have been used as a formidable stabbing weapon. The fifth finger was probably quite flexible — perhaps to manipulate food.

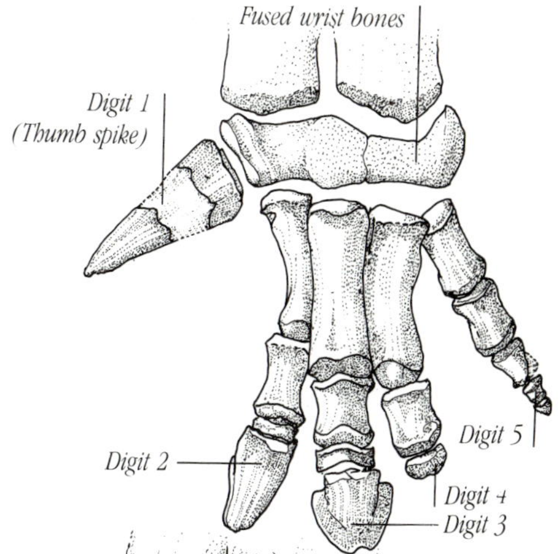

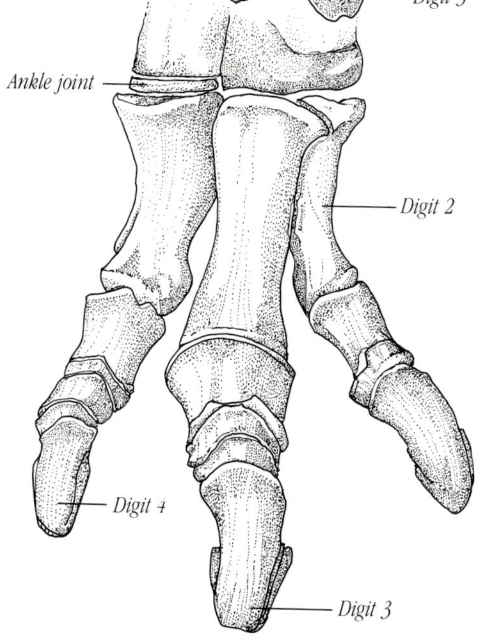

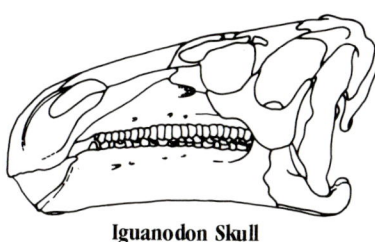

Iguanodon Skull

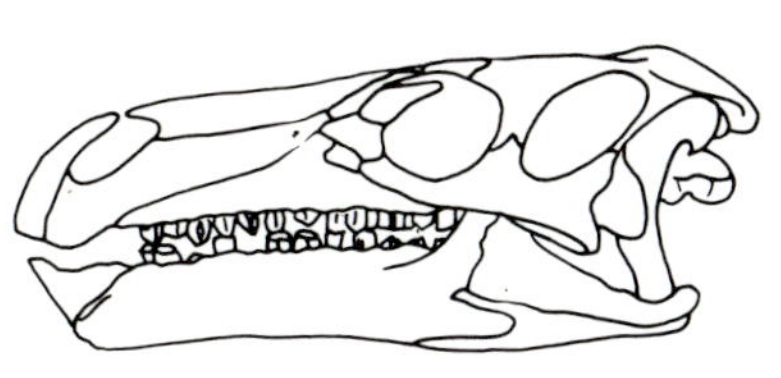

Camptosaurus Skull

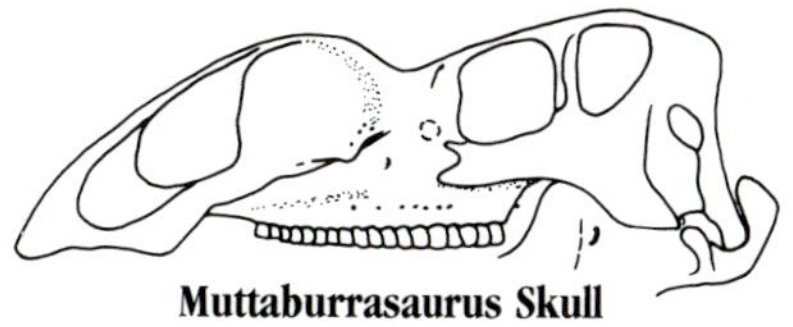

Muttaburrasaurus Skull

Skeleton Reconstructions (right)
Both *Ouranosaurus* (above) and *Iguanodon* (below) have fairly typical ornithopod skeletons. They are both bipedal, with the front legs reduced in size, but *Ouranosaurus* differs from the basic ornithopod plan in its large vertebral spines. They are both large animals, powerfully built compared with some ornithopods, and with particularly strong front legs. These may have been used in walking or resting on all-fours, rather like modern day kangaroos. This use of the front legs is quite different from that seen in the earlier ornithopods, and in fact iguanodontids are much more robust, less agile animals all round.

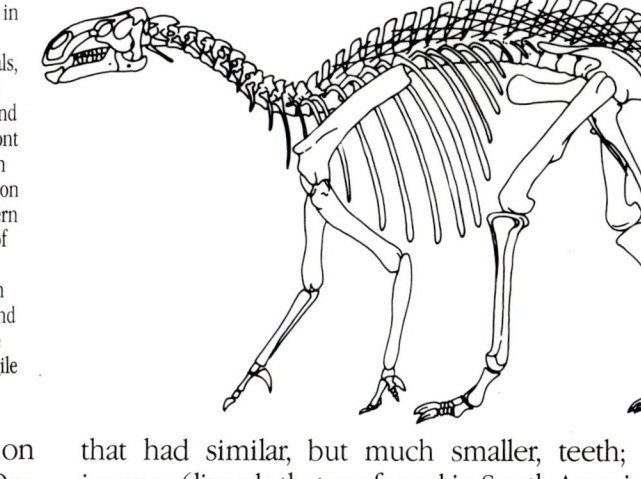

Iguanodon Skeleton

Iguanodon Foot (above)
This strong three-toed foot would have been necessary to support the weight of this large beast. Some of the individual toe bones have been much reduced in size, while the upper foot bones are fairly elongate and strong. *Iguanodon* probably walked on its toes like modern day cats and dogs.

Iguanodontids are larger than the hypsilophodontids on pages 26 and 27. Most seem to grow to a length of 7-9m (25-30ft). The earliest ones are found in rocks of late Jurassic age, but the remains of these sorts of dinosaur are found right through to the end of the Cretaceous Period. The group gets its name from the dinosaur named *Iguanodon* which can be seen in the foreground above.

Iguanodon (iguana tooth) is a very famous dinosaur because it was one of the first of all dinosaurs to be scientifically described. The first remains of this animal were found by Mary Ann Mantell, the wife of a doctor Gideon Algernon Mantell, a very keen collector of fossils who lived in Sussex, England in the early 1800s. The fossils that Mrs. Mantell found were several teeth, which Dr. Mantell had never seen before. After much careful searching, Dr. Mantell eventually found some living animals that had similar, but much smaller, teeth; these were iguanas (lizards that are found in South America). Because his fossil teeth were so big, Dr. Mantell gave them the name *Iguanodon* literally 'iguana tooth' thinking that his teeth probably belonged to a giant extinct relative of the living iguanas of South America.

Growing up to 9m (30ft) long, *Iguanodons* were large animals with strong back legs and large, three-toed feet. The footprints left by *Iguanodon* are very often found in the early Cretaceous rocks of southern England. The long, heavy tail balances the body over the hips and the front legs are not as long as the back ones, but are still quite strong. Its hands were equipped with a large spike-shaped thumb, offset from the hand. This was used for removing dust from the nose but more importantly, as a defensive weapon. When attacked, these animals were able to rear up and slash out with their hands at the faces of large theropod dinosaurs; a horrible weapon in a close fight. The three middle fingers had hooves so the hands could also be used for walking upon. The fifth finger was long and slender and probably used for picking up food.

The head of *Iguanodon* looks a little like that of a horse. It is quite large — 70-80cm (2.5ft) — with a horny beak at the front end for nipping off plants and many teeth along the sides of the jaws for crunching up the plants before they are swallowed.

Ouranosaurus (brave reptile) comes from the early Cretaceous rocks of Niger in Africa. Although smaller than *Iguanodon* — 7m (23ft) long — it is a very impressive animal because it has a row of tall spines that run down its back. Quite what these were for is not at all certain. The spines may have been used for display so that males could recognise females during the mating season, or so that males could recognise other rival males at this time of year. Another suggestion is that the spines could have worked rather like solar panels to warm up the dinosaurs' bodies during cold weather.

Camptosaurus (flexible reptile) comes from the late Jurassic Period of Wyoming and Colorado and was quite small at about 6.5m (20ft) long. It was very much like an earlier and smaller model of *Iguanodon*, although it does not have such a large spike on its thumb.

Muttaburrasaurus (reptile from Muttaburra) comes from the early Cretaceous of Australia but is, unfortunately, not very well known as yet. It seems to have been about the same size as *Ouranosaurus*, and had a large lump at the front of the snout between the nostrils. Quite what this was for is uncertain.

HADROSAURIDS I
Clockwise from top: Bactrosaurus, Kritosaurus, Edmontosaurus, Anatosaurus

Hadrosaurid Teeth (below)

Hadrosaurid jaws contain a formidable array of hundreds of teeth arranged in batteries on either side of both upper and lower jaws. These teeth acted like a rasping file and could deal with tough vegetation. The front end of the jaws was formed into a wide beak. The drawing below is a cross section through top and bottom jaws, showing how an up-and-down chewing action would cause the teeth to rub abrasively past one another and so crush the plant food. The drawing lower right is solely of the lower jaw. It clearly shows the tooth batteries.

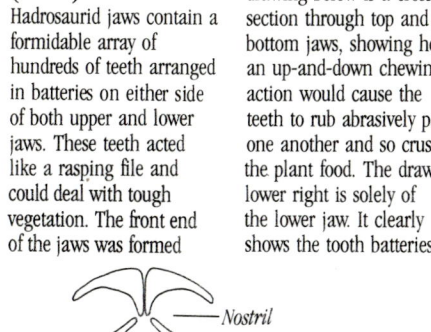

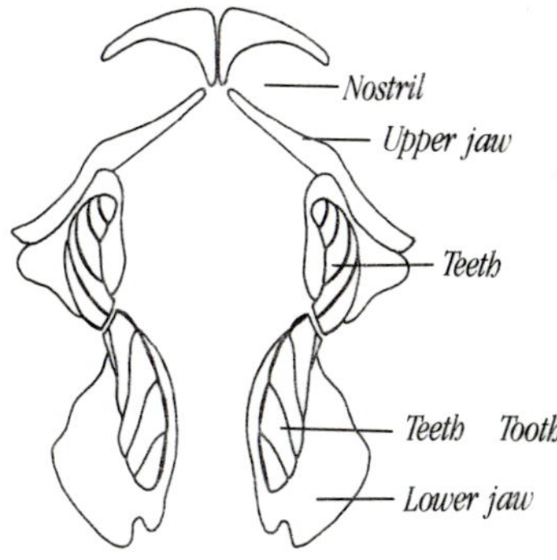

Hadrosaurid Skulls (right)

The skulls drawn here and on page 33 show the tremendous variety in the hadrosaurid skull. The three forms here belong to the 'hadrosaurines'. These had large duck-like beaks but little development of the crest, as you can see if you compare the regions coloured red here, which delineate the area of the nasal passages, with those on page 33. The back of the skull in all forms does not change very much which is surprising when you consider what is happening at the front! Even the three crestless forms here show some variation in their snouts: *Bactrosaurus* is very generalised, rather like an iguanodontid, *Kritosaurus* has an unusual bump on its nose and *Anatosaurus* has an extremely long, broad snout, which gave rise to the description 'duck-billed'.

Non-crested Hadrosaurid Pelvis / Crested Hadrosaurid Pelvis

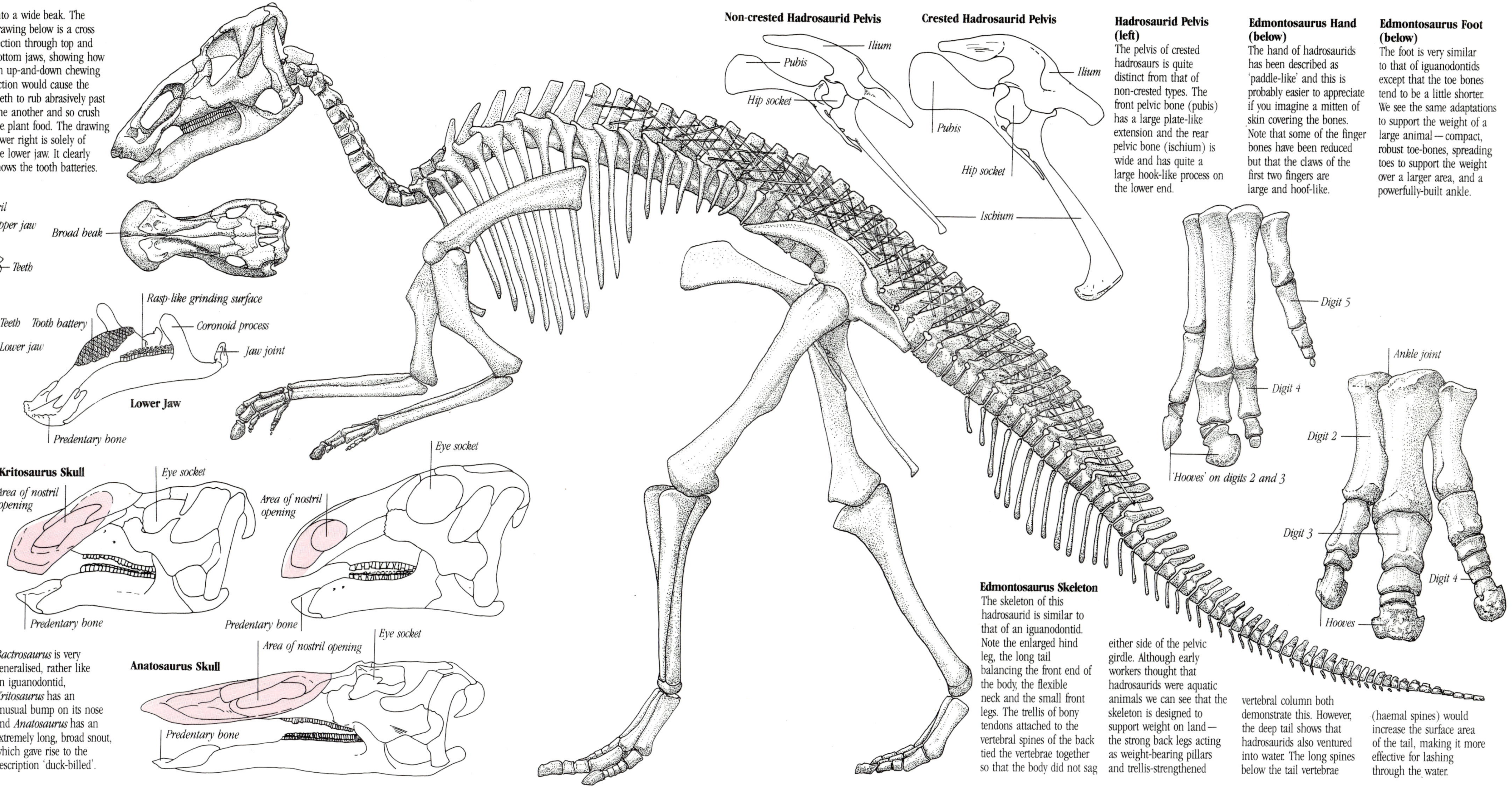

Hadrosaurid Pelvis (left)

The pelvis of crested hadrosaurs is quite distinct from that of non-crested types. The front pelvic bone (pubis) has a large plate-like extension and the rear pelvic bone (ischium) is wide and has quite a large hook-like process on the lower end.

Edmontosaurus Hand (below)

The hand of hadrosaurids has been described as 'paddle-like' and this is probably easier to appreciate if you imagine a mitten of skin covering the bones. Note that some of the finger bones have been reduced but that the claws of the first two fingers are large and hoof-like.

Edmontosaurus Foot (below)

The foot is very similar to that of iguanodontids except that the toe bones tend to be a little shorter. We see the same adaptations to support the weight of a large animal — compact, robust toe-bones, spreading toes to support the weight over a larger area, and a powerfully-built ankle.

Edmontosaurus Skeleton

The skeleton of this hadrosaurid is similar to that of an iguanodontid. Note the enlarged hind leg, the long tail balancing the front end of the body, the flexible neck and the small front legs. The trellis of bony tendons attached to the vertebral spines of the back tied the vertebrae together so that the body did not sag either side of the pelvic girdle. Although early workers thought that hadrosaurids were aquatic animals we can see that the skeleton is designed to support weight on land — the strong back legs acting as weight-bearing pillars and trellis-strengthened vertebral column both demonstrate this. However, the deep tail shows that hadrosaurids also ventured into water. The long spines below the tail vertebrae (haemal spines) would increase the surface area of the tail, making it more effective for lashing through the water.

The hadrosaurids were the last group of ornithopods to appear. The earliest ones come from the middle of the Cretaceous Period. Although they only lasted until the end of the Cretaceous Period, which is when all the other dinosaurs died out too, the hadrosaurids did become surprisingly varied in appearance and very abundant, judging by the large number of fossils of these animals that have been found in many parts of the world. As a group, they grew to about the same size as the iguanodontids (see previous page) although there are one or two examples of larger ones. For example, a Chinese hadrosaurid — *Shantungosaurus* — grew to a length of 12m (39ft) and some *Edmontosaurus* specimens from Canada are supposed to have reached a length of 13m (42ft). All the early discoveries of hadrosaurids were made in the USA where, from the 1850s onwards, various fragmentary fossils were found, quite often during the building of the American railroads.

The hadrosaurids are very similar in almost all their characteristics to the iguanodontids. The bodies of the two groups were almost the same in shape, with large back legs and long muscular tails and slightly smaller front legs. One difference that can be seen is that hadrosaurids only have four fingers on the hand. For some reason hadrosaurids seem to have been able to cope without the defensive thumb spike for fighting off theropods. Perhaps they were better at running and could escape more easily from the big meat eaters like the tyrannosaurids.

These dinosaurs are also often called 'duck billed dinosaurs', which refers to another feature that is peculiar to this group; the rather broad, duck-like beak that many of them have (see *Anatosaurus* in particular).

The hadrosaurids that we are looking at on these pages are known as 'hadrosaurine' or, more simply, as flat-headed hadrosaurs. You can see why if you compare them to those on the next page!

Bactrosaurus (reptile from Bactria) is one of the earliest hadrosaurs known; it comes from the middle Cretaceous rocks of Mongolia. It is quite small by the standard of most hadrosaurs at 6m (20ft) long. Unlike later hadrosaurs, it does not seem to have had the broad duck-like beak, but one much more like that of the iguanodontids. However it did have a huge number of teeth for chewing up tough plants.

Edmontosaurus (reptile from Edmonton, Alberta) is a large hadrosaur and is very typical of this group of dinosaurs. The thin bony rods that stiffened the tail can be seen clearly along the sides of the spines on the skeleton drawing above.

The skull of *Edmontosaurus* is large and has a very wide beak. Behind the beak are an enormously large number of teeth which make a great big grinding area for mashing up plants before swallowing them. These special grinding teeth allowed these dinosaurs to eat tough plants which other dinosaurs with weaker teeth were unable to chew.

Anatosaurus (duck reptile) is named this for the very obvious reason that its big flat beak makes it look like a gigantic duck! Above the beak it had very large nostrils and it is thought that these were used not only for sniffing with but also for making loud noises, rather like the elephant seals of today, who make loud roaring sounds, especially during the mating season.

Kritosaurus (chosen reptile) is similar to the hadrosaurs listed above, but has a peculiar lump on its nose, which makes it look a little like *Muttaburrasaurus* (pages 28-29).

HADROSAURIDS II
From left to right: Tsintaosaurus, Saurolophus, Corythosaurus, Parasaurolophus

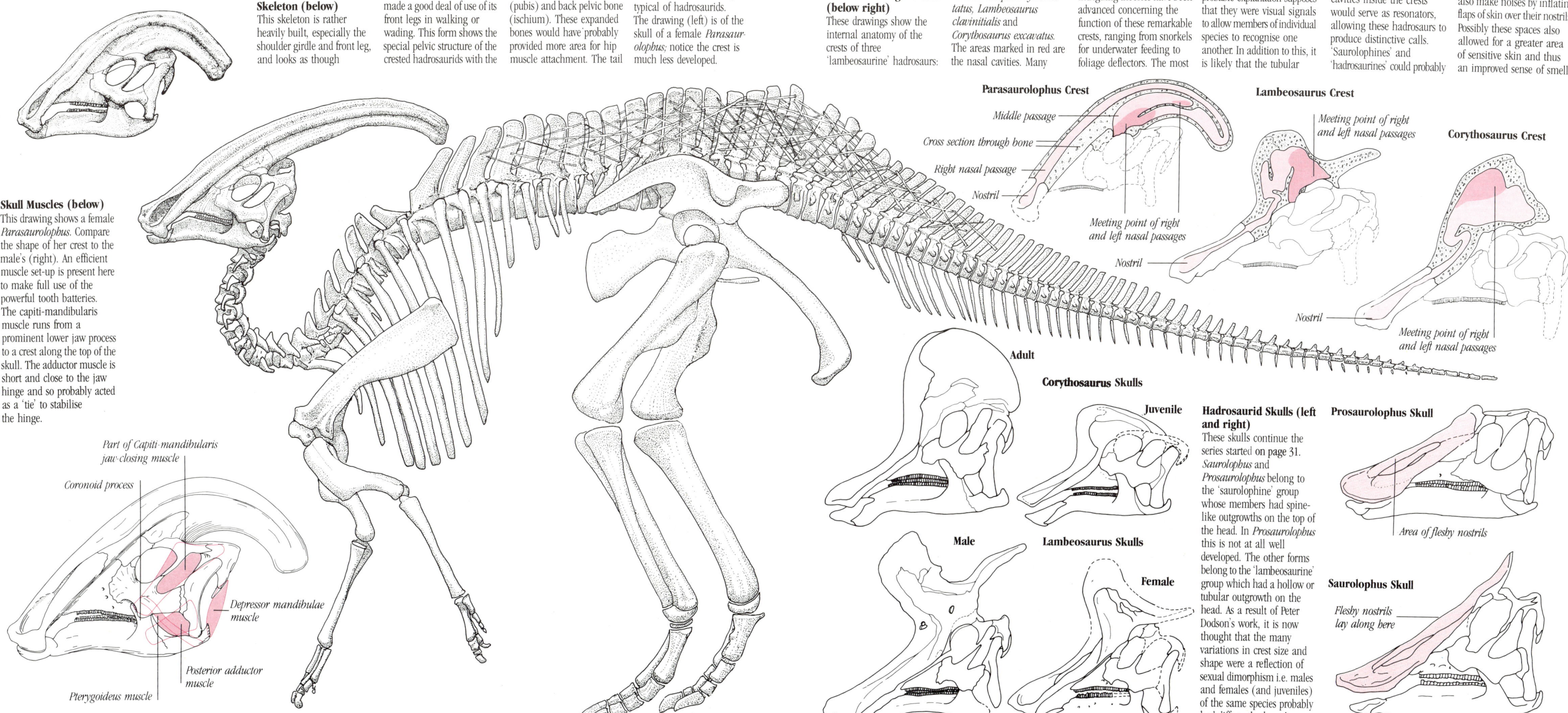

Female Parasaurolophus Skull

Parasaurolophus Skeleton (below) This skeleton is rather heavily built, especially the shoulder girdle and front leg, and looks as though *Parasaurolophus* would have made a good deal of use of its front legs in walking or wading. This form shows the special pelvic structure of the crested hadrosaurids with the enlarged front pelvic bone (pubis) and back pelvic bone (ischium). These expanded bones would have probably provided more area for hip muscle attachment. The tail here shows the flattening typical of hadrosaurids. The drawing (left) is of the skull of a female *Parasaurolophus*; notice the crest is much less developed.

Sections through Crests (below right) These drawings show the internal anatomy of the crests of three 'lambeosaurine' hadrosaurs: *Parasaurolophus cyrtocristatus*, *Lambeosaurus clavinitialis* and *Corythosaurus excavatus*. The areas marked in red are the nasal cavities. Many intriguing theories have been advanced concerning the function of these remarkable crests, ranging from snorkels for underwater feeding to foliage deflectors. The most probable explanation supposes that they were visual signals to allow members of individual species to recognise one another. In addition to this, it is likely that the tubular cavities inside the crests would serve as resonators, allowing these hadrosaurs to produce distinctive calls. 'Saurolophines' and 'hadrosaurines' could probably also make noises by inflating flaps of skin over their nostrils. Possibly these spaces also allowed for a greater area of sensitive skin and thus an improved sense of smell.

Skull Muscles (below) This drawing shows a female *Parasaurolophus*. Compare the shape of her crest to the male's (right). An efficient muscle set-up is present here to make full use of the powerful tooth batteries. The capiti-mandibularis muscle runs from a prominent lower jaw process to a crest along the top of the skull. The adductor muscle is short and close to the jaw hinge and so probably acted as a 'tie' to stabilise the hinge.

Hadrosaurid Skulls (left and right) These skulls continue the series started on page 31. *Saurolophus* and *Prosaurolophus* belong to the 'saurolophine' group whose members had spine-like outgrowths on the top of the head. In *Prosaurolophus* this is not at all well developed. The other forms belong to the 'lambeosaurine' group which had a hollow or tubular outgrowth on the head. As a result of Peter Dodson's work, it is now thought that the many variations in crest size and shape were a reflection of sexual dimorphism i.e. males and females (and juveniles) of the same species probably had differently shaped crests.

The other main group of hadrosaurs are rather more exotic than the first ones that we looked at on pages 30-31. They are often referred to as 'lambeosaurine' instead of 'hadrosaurine'. This name derives from the dinosaur *Lambeosaurus* which had a large crest on the top of its head (see above). In general, the bodies of all these dinosaurs are very similar to the ones that have already been described; their main characteristic is that they have some most peculiar head-gear.

Parasaurolophus (parallel crested reptile) is one of the more unusual of all the lambeosaurine hadrosaurs. Compared to many of the other hadrosaurs its remains are quite rare and have only been found in North America. It grew to a length of about 10m (35ft).

The crest on its head is as much as 1m (3ft) long in some examples and is made up of two hollow tubes, one on top of the other and joined at the far end. The front end of the tubes join up with the nostrils. What was this crest for? There have been a number of theories in the past. Until quite recently, one of the most widely held ideas was that the crest was used as a type of breathing tube, or snorkel, when the head of the animal was under water. This would enable it to feed on water weeds while breathing through a hole in the far end of the crest. Nice though this idea was, it is not feasible because there is no hole at the far end of the crest! The most likely theory, and the one that is accepted by most scientists today, is that the tubes were similar to the pipes of a trombone and were used to produce a very distinctive hooting noise. It has been suggested that these dinosaurs may have lived in rather dense undergrowth in forests and may have called to one another, using their crests, to keep in touch.

Corythosaurus (Corinthian's helmet reptile), again from North America, has a narrower and higher crest than *Parasaurolophus* with a differently shaped inner hollow region. Another idea that was put forward quite recently was that the crest was a way of allowing these animals to improve their sense of smell, the theory being the bigger your nose, the better your sense of smell!

Lambeosaurus, named after Lawrence Lambe, a Canadian dinosaur expert, comes from Canada and has a crest that looks rather similar to that of *Corythosaurus* except that it has a backwardly-pointing spike as well as the helmet-shaped crest.

Both *Corythosaurus* and *Lambeosaurus* show fossils that do not look quite the same. Some have larger crests than others, and it is now thought that these differences may be because some are male while others are female.

Saurolophus (crested reptile) and **Prosaurolophus** (early crested reptile) both have rather flat faces and a small upturned spike or ridge above the eyes. This leaves a large flat area over the nose, which may well have been covered in inflatable skin for use as a resonator for honking at other members of the species.

Tsintaosaurus (reptile from Tsintao) is one of a small number of Chinese dinosaurs. This one is remarkable because of the strange spike that rises from its head rather like the horn of the legendary unicorn.

While it cannot be doubted that these dinosaurs were land living for much of their lives, there are some remarkable fossil skeletons of hadrosaurs which are preserved as 'mummies' with parts of their skin. These show that hadrosaurs had a mitten on their hands for swimming.

Psittacosaurs & Protoceratopids
Protoceratops (left) and Psittacosaurus

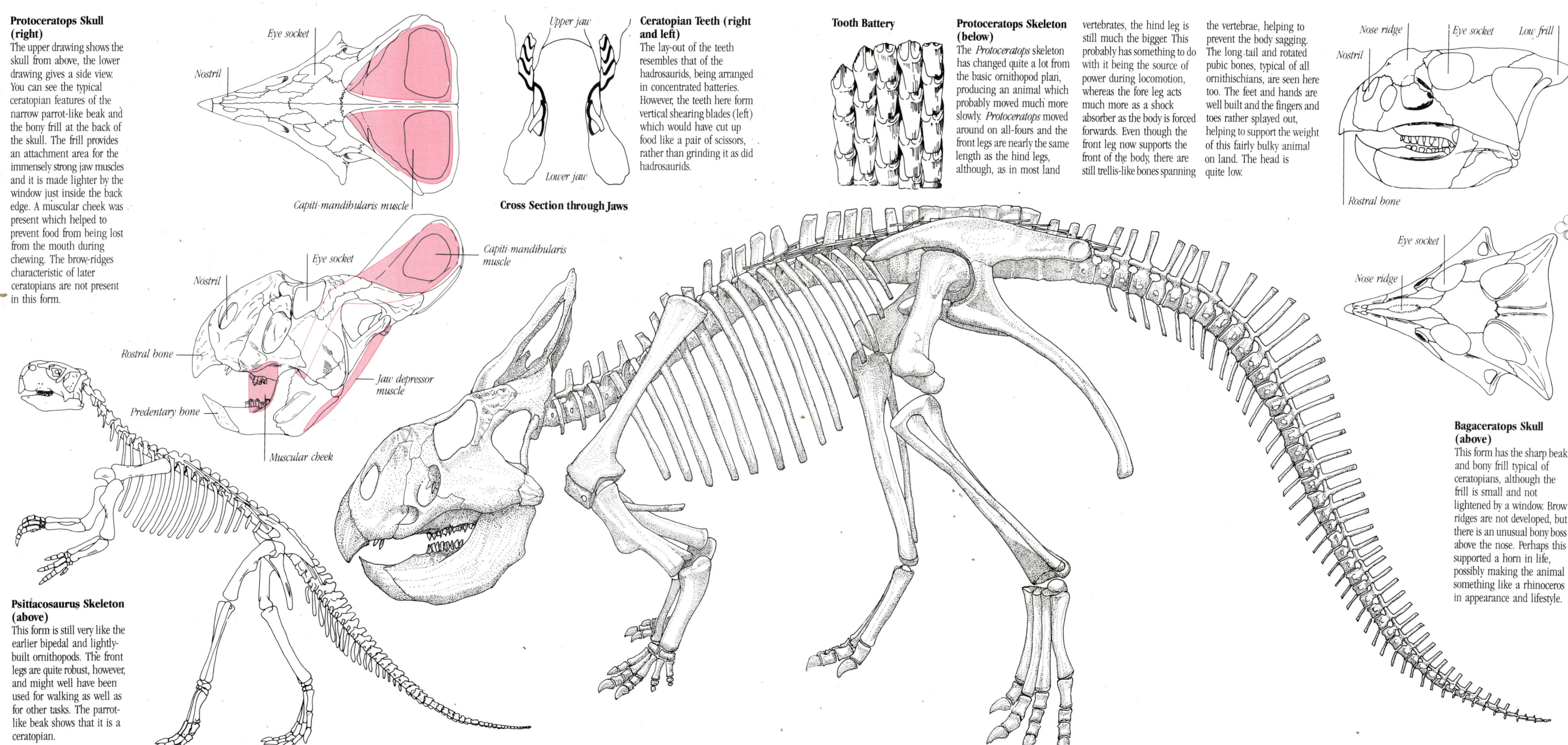

Protoceratops Skull (right)
The upper drawing shows the skull from above, the lower drawing gives a side view. You can see the typical ceratopian features of the narrow parrot-like beak and the bony frill at the back of the skull. The frill provides an attachment area for the immensely strong jaw muscles and it is made lighter by the window just inside the back edge. A muscular cheek was present which helped to prevent food from being lost from the mouth during chewing. The brow-ridges characteristic of later ceratopians are not present in this form.

Ceratopian Teeth (right and left)
The lay-out of the teeth resembles that of the hadrosaurids, being arranged in concentrated batteries. However, the teeth here form vertical shearing blades (left) which would have cut up food like a pair of scissors, rather than grinding it as did hadrosaurids.

Protoceratops Skeleton (below)
The *Protoceratops* skeleton has changed quite a lot from the basic ornithopod plan, producing an animal which probably moved much more slowly. *Protoceratops* moved around on all-fours and the front legs are nearly the same length as the hind legs, although, as in most land vertebrates, the hind leg is still much the bigger. This probably has something to do with it being the source of power during locomotion, whereas the fore leg acts much more as a shock absorber as the body is forced forwards. Even though the front leg now supports the front of the body, there are still trellis-like bones spanning the vertebrae, helping to prevent the body sagging. The long tail and rotated pubic bones, typical of all ornithischians, are seen here too. The feet and hands are well built and the fingers and toes rather splayed out, helping to support the weight of this fairly bulky animal on land. The head is quite low.

Bagaceratops Skull (above)
This form has the sharp beak and bony frill typical of ceratopians, although the frill is small and not lightened by a window. Brow ridges are not developed, but there is an unusual bony boss above the nose. Perhaps this supported a horn in life, possibly making the animal something like a rhinoceros in appearance and lifestyle.

Psittacosaurus Skeleton (above)
This form is still very like the earlier bipedal and lightly-built ornithopods. The front legs are quite robust, however, and might well have been used for walking as well as for other tasks. The parrot-like beak shows that it is a ceratopian.

The ceratopian group of dinosaurs, to which both of these types of dinosaur belong, only arose right at the end of the reign of the dinosaurs, that is at the end of the Cretaceous Period. However, even though they were rather late on the scene, they did become incredibly abundant. In some places in North America, hundreds of bones of these sorts of animals can be found, as well as a few complete skeletons. The really distinctive feature of all ceratopian dinosaurs is the narrow, parrot-like beak at the front of the mouth (see above and pages 36-39). The psittacosaurs and protoceratopids are not like the majority of ceratopians and are shown here on their own.

Psittacosaurus (parrot reptile) is a small to medium sized ceratopian, none of which seemed to grow larger than about 2m (6ft) in length. All the remains of this type of dinosaur are found in middle Cretaceous rocks in Mongolia and China. One very poorly preserved skeleton has been reported from Germany, but it is difficult to be sure that its identification is correct.

The first fossils of this animal were discovered in Mongolia in the 1920s during an expedition that was organised by the American Museum of New York. The fossils brought back included two almost complete skeletons as well as lots of other fragments, including parts of some baby *Psittacosaurus*.

Unlike just about all other ceratopians, these were built like ornithopod dinosaurs. They had strong back legs and a long tail, which helped to balance the body over the hips, and the front legs were quite short, but powerful with strongly clawed hands. The neck was of normal length (unlike most ceratopians which have extremely short necks) and the head, even though it was short and chunky, with a parrot-like beak, does not have either the prominent frill over the neck, or the horns found in so many others.

One strange discovery was that one of the skeletons that was brought back from Mongolia had a large pile of stones crammed into the area where the stomach of the animal would have been. This was no accident. These are what are known as stomach stones or gastroliths, to give them their technical name. They were deliberately swallowed by *Psittacosaurus*, in the same way that birds swallow grit, so that they can feed properly. The stones are kept in the stomach and are used to pound up the plant food so that it can be digested more easily.

Protoceratops (first horned-face) were again fairly small, 2m (6ft) long creatures, about the same size as *Psittacosaurus*. Unlike *Psittacosaurus* however, *Protoceratops* walked on four legs rather than just its back ones, and it had a much larger and more ornate head. It was rather like a miniature version of some of the large ceratopians that we shall be looking at in the next few pages.

Protoceratops was also found on the famous American Museum expedition to Mongolia of the 1920s, and again, many skeletons were discovered including the remains of young or baby ones. Not only were these fossils discovered but, more exciting at the time, was the discovery of the very first nests of dinosaur eggs that belong to these dinosaurs. Many of these nests were well preserved and they were, for a long time, the best examples of dinosaur eggs and nests until the more recent discovery of hadrosaurid (pages 30-33) nest sites in Montana, by John Horner.

Several other protoceratopian dinosaurs have been discovered in Mongolia in recent years of which **Bagaceratops** (small horned face) is an example.

CERATOPIDS I
From top to bottom: Styracosaurus, Theeratops, Centrosaurus

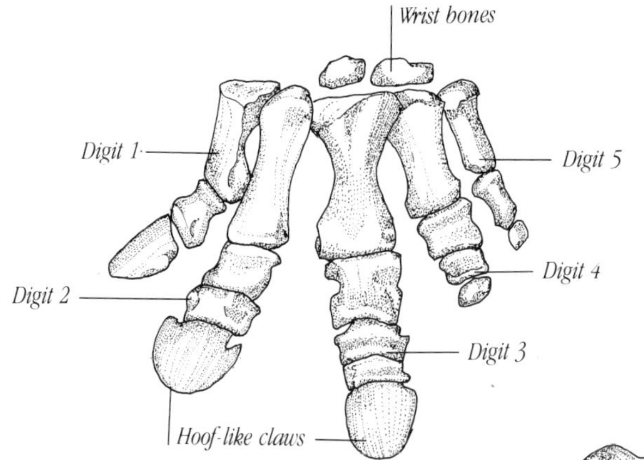

Wrist bones

Centrosaurus Hand (left)
This strong, stubby hand is exactly what you would expect to find in a large, heavy animal. It is clear that such an animal would not be able to run particularly fast, and *Centrosaurus* presumably dealt with predators using the 'fight' rather than the 'flight' strategy! Notice how the finger bones are short but wide, and that they are capped with strong hoof-like claws, particularly on the middle fingers.

Digit 1, *Digit 2*, *Digit 3*, *Digit 4*, *Digit 5*, *Hoof-like claws*

Centrosaurus Foot (right)
The foot also shows that its owner was a large beast that did not rely on speed to get it out of danger. The four toes are all strong but fairly short, and like the fingers they are splayed out to provide a greater surface area over which to take the animal's considerable weight. As the posture of the main skeleton indicates, this form probably walked up on its toes, rather than on its whole foot.

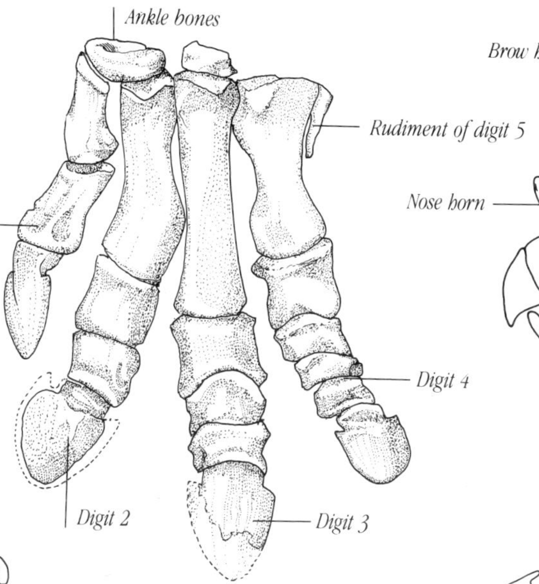

Ankle bones, *Digit 1*, *Digit 2*, *Digit 3*, *Digit 4*

Triceratops Skull
Brow horn, *Rudiment of digit 5*, *Nostril*, *Nose horn*, *Eye socket*, *Epoccipital bones*

Slots for jaw muscles

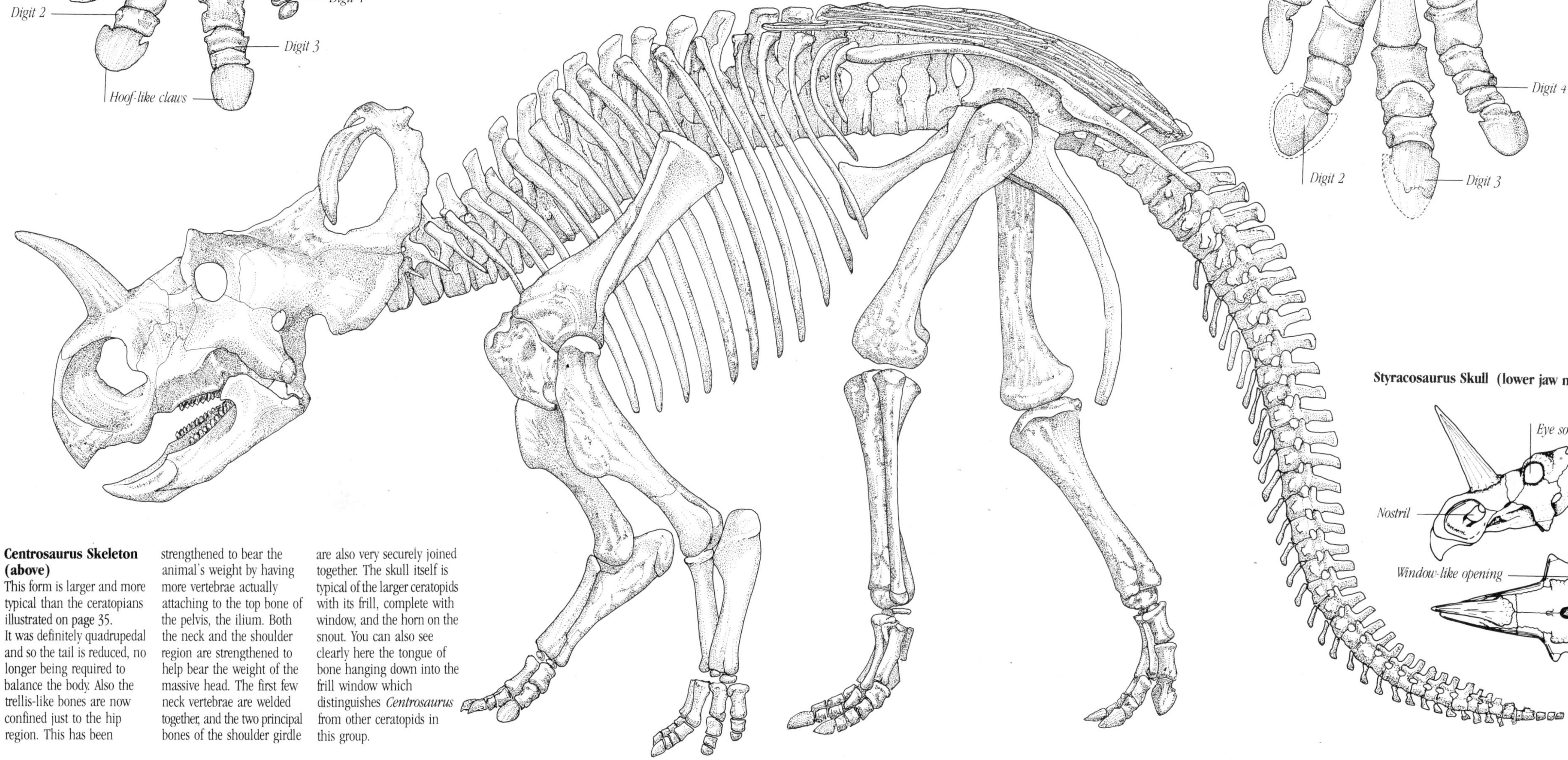

Styracosaurus Skull (lower jaw missing)
Eye socket, *Epoccipital bones*, *Nostril*, *Window-like opening*, *Roof of brain case nearly closed over*

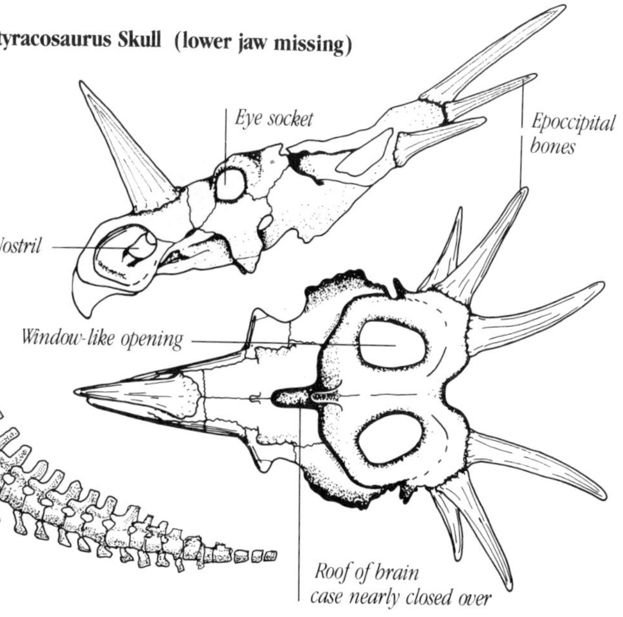

Triceratops Skull (above)
The forms illustrated on this page are all short-frilled ceratopids. *Triceratops* has a short, solid frill encircled by a series of epoccipital bones giving the frill its characteristic wavy edge. The brow horns are large and the nose horn small.

Styracosaurus Skull (left)
This form is distinguished by its characteristic frill in which the epoccipital bones have been drawn out into long spikes. Rather than being purely defensive these may have provided behavioural signals for rivals or to attract mates.

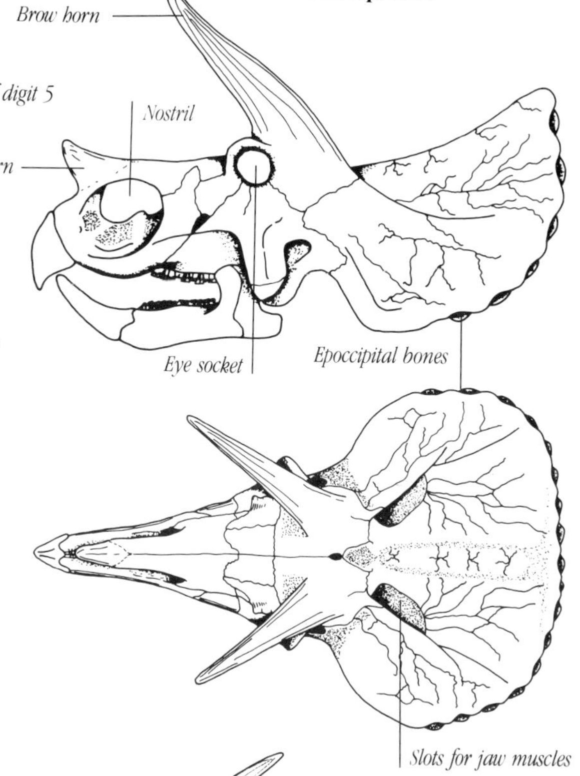

Centrosaurus Skeleton (above)
This form is larger and more typical than the ceratopians illustrated on page 35. It was definitely quadrupedal and so the tail is reduced, no longer being required to balance the body. Also the trellis-like bones are now confined just to the hip region. This has been strengthened to bear the animal's weight by having more vertebrae actually attaching to the top bone of the pelvis, the ilium. Both the neck and the shoulder region are strengthened to help bear the weight of the massive head. The first few neck vertebrae are welded together, and the two principal bones of the shoulder girdle are also very securely joined together. The skull itself is typical of the larger ceratopids with its frill, complete with window, and the horn on the snout. You can also see clearly here the tongue of bone hanging down into the frill window which distinguishes *Centrosaurus* from other ceratopids in this group.

The larger and more typical ceratopian dinosaurs were first found in the 1850s in Montana, but these fossils were all very poor specimens that meant hardly anything to the scientists who looked at them. We only realise what they are now that newer discoveries have been made. It was not until the late 1880s that the first well preserved material was found, this time in Niobrara County, Wyoming. John Hatcher, who later became a famous American dinosaur expert, discovered these fossils and, in fact, on his first expedition to the area found a complete skull of *Triceratops*. Over the next few years Hatcher went on to discover more than 30 skeletons of these ceratopians, some complete but many rather broken. Up to the present day all of the fossils of ceratopids have been found in North America; none have come from anywhere else in the world, even Asia where the early types of dinosaurs such as *Psittacosaurus* and *Protoceratops* have been found.

The ceratopids featured in this section are what could be called the short-frilled types. If they are compared with the ceratopids on pages 38-39 it will be obvious that the ones featured here have much shorter frills behind the head and also tend to have rather larger nose horns.

Triceratops (three-horned face) is an extremely well-known dinosaur which is known from rocks of the very latest Cretaceous Period, quite close to the time of extinction of all the dinosaurs. It was one of the largest of all the ceratopids, reaching a length of about 9m (29ft). This does not sound particularly large by dinosaur standards, but ceratopians are not typical dinosaurs. Nearly all other dinosaurs have a very long tail that helps to make them appear to be very long. Ceratopians however, do not have a particularly large tail and it was certainly not used, as in ornithopods for example, to balance the body at the hips. So these dinosaurs are really very bulky animals with a heavy body and a massive bony head.

The nearest equivalent to *Triceratops* living today must be the rhinoceros of Africa. Both are heavy-headed, four footed animals, with large horns. The *Triceratops* would have been more than a match for the tyrannosaurids (pages 14-15) that were the main large meat eaters of the time.

Centrosaurus (sharp point reptile) from Canada and the USA is a slightly smaller type of ceratopid than the *Triceratops*, reaching a length of 6m (20ft). The body of all these animals is very similar, the differences being found in the skull. In the case of *Centrosaurus*, the differences are obvious. The horn on the nose is very large and sticks upwards; the eyebrow horns are very small, while those of *Triceratops* are big; the frill has large holes in it and there are banana-shaped bones that point downward into these holes for the attachment of the very large jaw muscles.

Centrosaurus is well known in Canada. There are some places where it is almost impossible to find any other fossils than the bones of *Centrosaurus*.

Styracosaurus (spiked reptile), again from Canada, has a most unusual skull. At first sight the frill seems to be very long, but this is an illusion, because it is really quite small; what makes it appear big is the row of long spikes that stick out from its edge. If you look carefully at the edge of the frill in *Triceratops* (above) you will see lots of little epoccipital bones; it is these that have grown very large in *Styracosaurus*. Quite why these bones should have grown so big is uncertain, but it could well have something to do with members of the species recognising one another.

CERATOPIDS II
From left to right: Chasmosaurus, Torosaurus, Anchiceratops, Pentaceratops

Torosaurus Skull (lower jaw missing)

Eye socket
Nostril
Smooth-edged frill

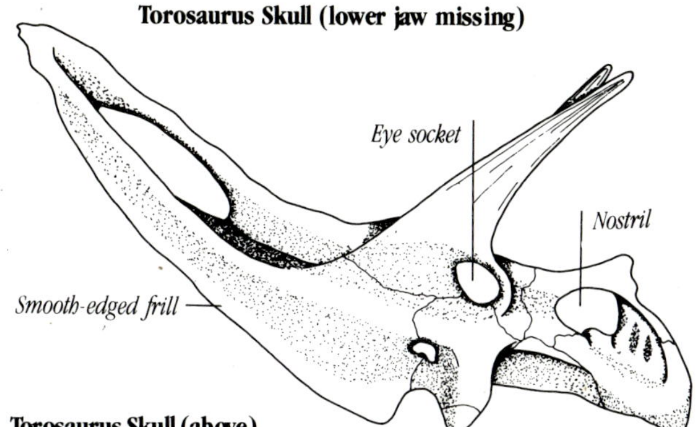

Torosaurus Skull (above)
Here we see typical long-frilled ceratopid features: the extensive frill, large brow horns and smaller nasal horn. But we also see the specialised features of *Torosaurus*—the frill is rather low and lacks epoccipital bones giving it a very smooth outline, and its windows are rather small.

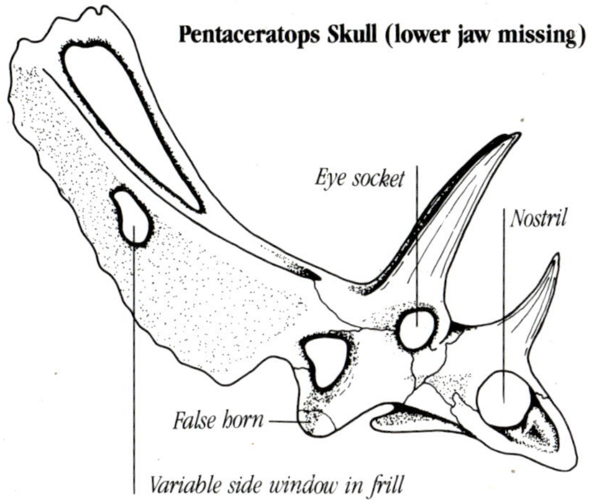

Pentaceratops Skull (right)
To live up to its name this form should have five horns, but in fact the so-called cheek horns are really just elongated bones and they can also be seen in other species. As in all the long-frilled forms *Pentaceratops* has a long, low face and a tapering muzzle.

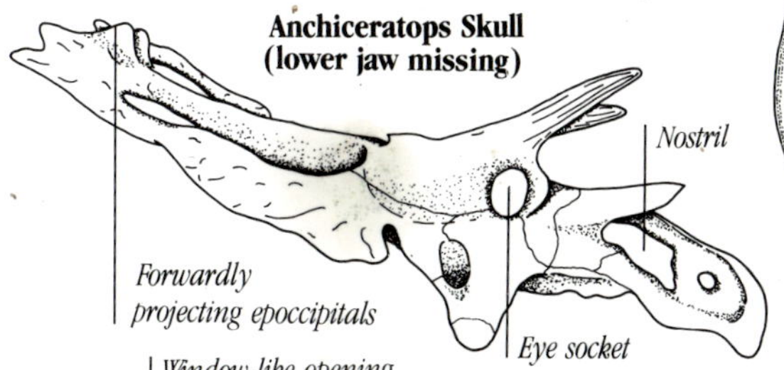

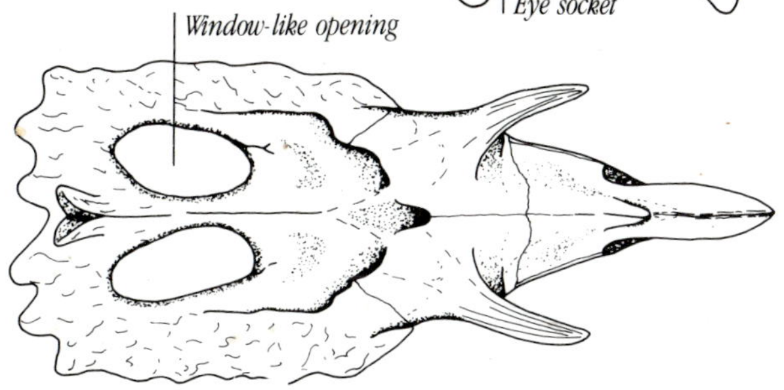

Anchiceratops Skull (right)
This form has a very distinctive frill structure although its face is very much like that of other ceratopids. The frill windows are quite small and its back is edged by three pairs of large epoccipitals. Two of these bones also project forwards from the back edge of the skull. The eyebrow horns are very long and pointed.

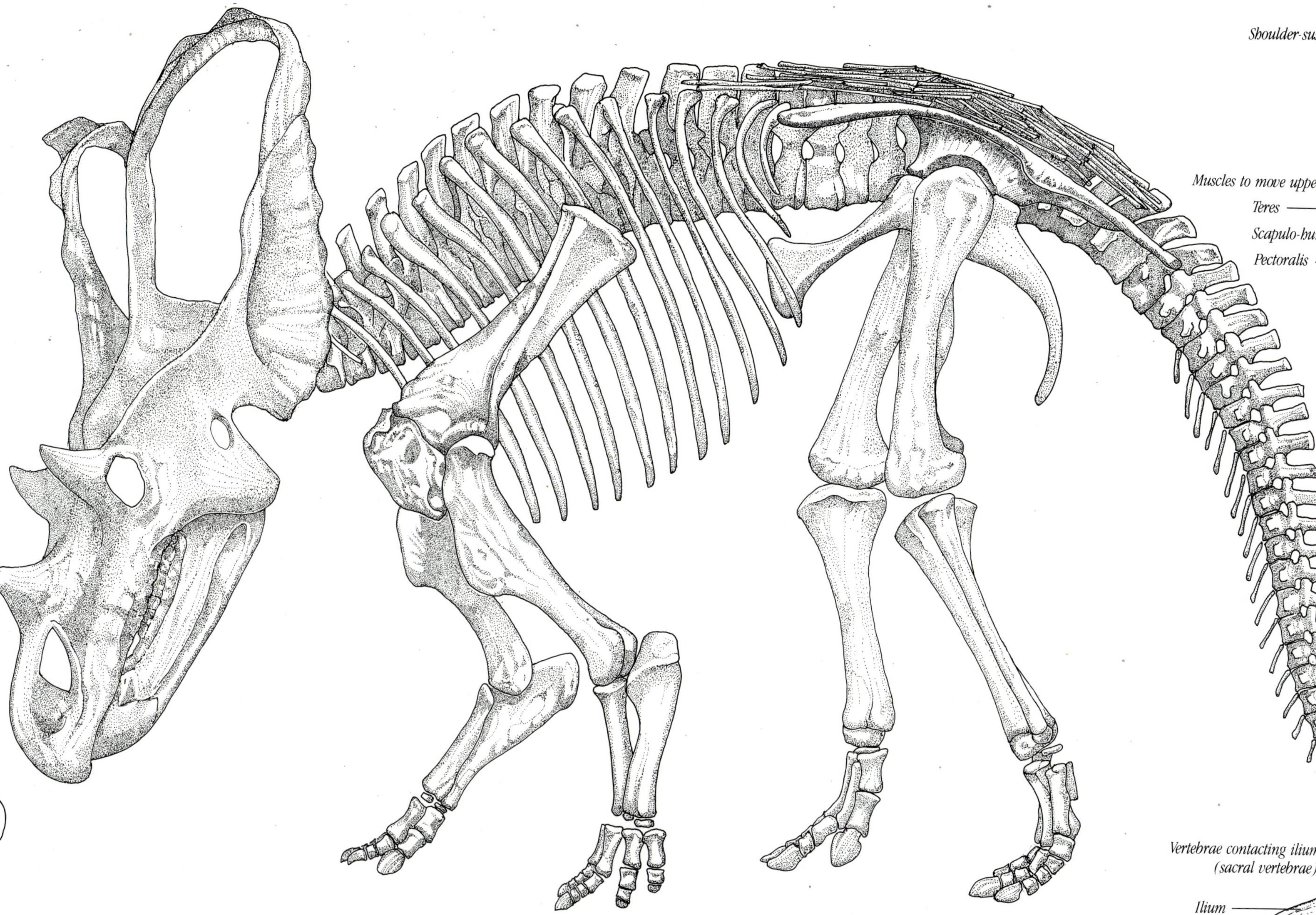

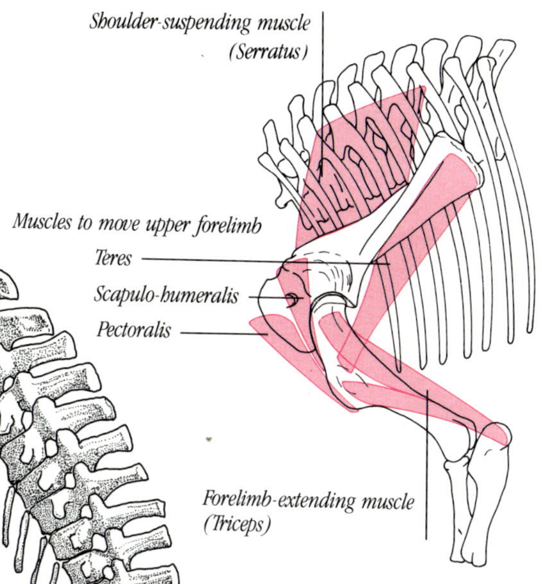

Pentaceratops Skull (lower jaw missing)

Eye socket
Nostril
False horn
Variable side window in frill

Anchiceratops Skull (lower jaw missing)

Forwardly projecting epoccipitals
Nostril
Eye socket
Window-like opening

Chasmosaurus Skeleton (above)
This skeleton is typical of a large, lumbering reptile. Both the hip and shoulder girdles, as well as their respective legs, are very solidly built—designed for weight-bearing, not speed. The vertebrae are also very large and strong, especially in the neck and back regions. Here they have extensive spines to which head-supporting muscles attach. The ribs are also stout. These would have helped to support the bulky gut which such a hefty animal would have needed to process large amounts of food. In the skull notice the small blunt brow horns—they are typical of *Chasmosaurus belli*.

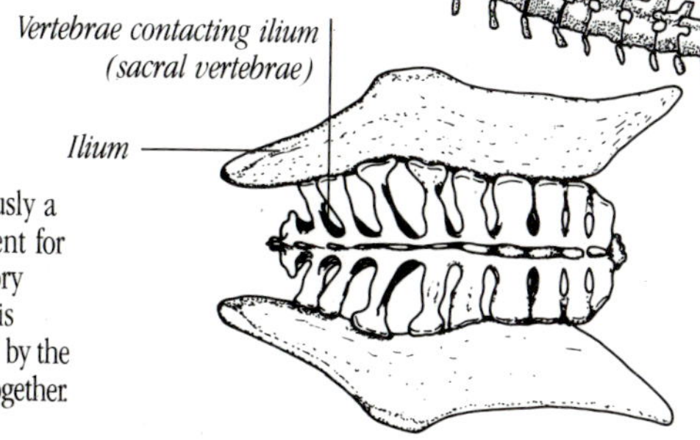

Chasmosaurus Pelvis (right)
This is a view of the pelvis from above the animal's back. At least eight vertebrae contact each upper pelvic bone (ilium)—obviously a very strong arrangement for transmitting locomotory forces. Extra strength is provided in this region by the vertebrae being fused together.

Chasmosaurus Shoulder (above)
Some of the muscles responsible for stabilising the shoulder and moving the front leg are shown here. The serratus muscle suspends the shoulder blade from the vertebral column—there is no bony connection here. The triceps extends the forearm and the other muscles move the upper arm up, down, backwards or forwards.

Shoulder-suspending muscle (Serratus)
Muscles to move upper forelimb
Teres
Scapulo-humeralis
Pectoralis
Forelimb-extending muscle (Triceps)
Vertebrae contacting ilium (sacral vertebrae)
Ilium

The other group of ceratopids are the long-frilled ones. As can be seen in the picture, the frill, which was like a ruff on the neck, was very large indeed and often decorated with spikes or bumps, giving it a distinctive shape. Looking at the skeleton, it is almost identical to that of the short-frilled ceratopids seen on pages 36-37. Just as in the case of the ornithopods, nearly all of the differences between these two groups of dinosaurs seem to be in the shape of the head.

Torosaurus (bull reptile) in the foreground above, comes from Wyoming and is almost typical of all the long-frilled ceratopids. The frill of this creature is well over 1.6m (5ft) long, stretching way back over the shoulders and chest of the animal. The entire head of the *Torosaurus* is 2.6m (8.5ft) long and is the largest head of any known land-living animal. Above the eyes there are two large horns and a much smaller one on the nose. The beak is large and parrot-like with sharp, curved cutting edges for slicing off pieces of vegetation. Behind the beak are the teeth which, as can be seen on page 35, are arranged to form cutting edges like a pair of scissors. The jaws must have worked to cut the plants into short pieces before they were swallowed. While the food was being chewed, it was held in the mouth by cheeks which stopped it falling out of the sides. Living reptiles do not have cheeks, yet many plant eating dinosaurs seem to have had them. If you look back at the pictures of most of the ornithischian dinosaurs you will find that they have been drawn with cheeks. The saurischian plant eaters did not chew food in their mouths so they did not need cheeks.

Chasmosaurus (cleft reptile) from Alberta grew to a length of about 5m (17ft) and was rather smaller than *Torosaurus* which, although it is only known at the moment from the gigantic skull must have been about 8m (25ft) long. Several very fine skeletons of *Chasmosaurus* are known. Again its characteristic features are to be found on its skull and frill. Its eyebrow horns tend to be a lot shorter than other long-frilled types, and the edge of its frill tends to be decorated with small pointed epoccipital bones along the sides and at the top corners.

Chasmosaurus was one of the earliest of the long-frilled dinosaurs, while *Torosaurus* was one of the last that lived right at the end of the reign of the dinosaurs.

Anchiceratops (close-horned face) again from Alberta, was just a little bit larger than *Chasmosaurus*. It had quite large eyebrow horns compared to *Chasmosaurus* and a very distinctive pair of small forward-pointing epoccipital bones situated at the middle, near the top of the frill.

Pentaceratops (five-horned face) from New Mexico was slightly larger again than *Anchiceratops* measuring some 7m (23ft) from head to tail. It was given the name 'five-horned face' because it was thought that it really did have five horns instead of the usual three. If you look carefully you will see that there are only three horns as usual—the scientists got it wrong! They thought that the very prominent cheek bones were horns as well, but if you look at other ceratopids you will see that they all have pointed cheek bones. The only real distinguishing feature is the even row of epoccipital bones that fringe the entire frill.

The frill in ceratopian dinosaurs must have been very important to them or it would not have been so large. It was probably used as a place to anchor the huge jaw muscles that these animals had and also in conjunction with the horns as a part of their behaviour for fighting and display.

PACHYCEPHALOSAURS

From left to right: Homalocephale, Pachycephalosaurus, Stegoceras

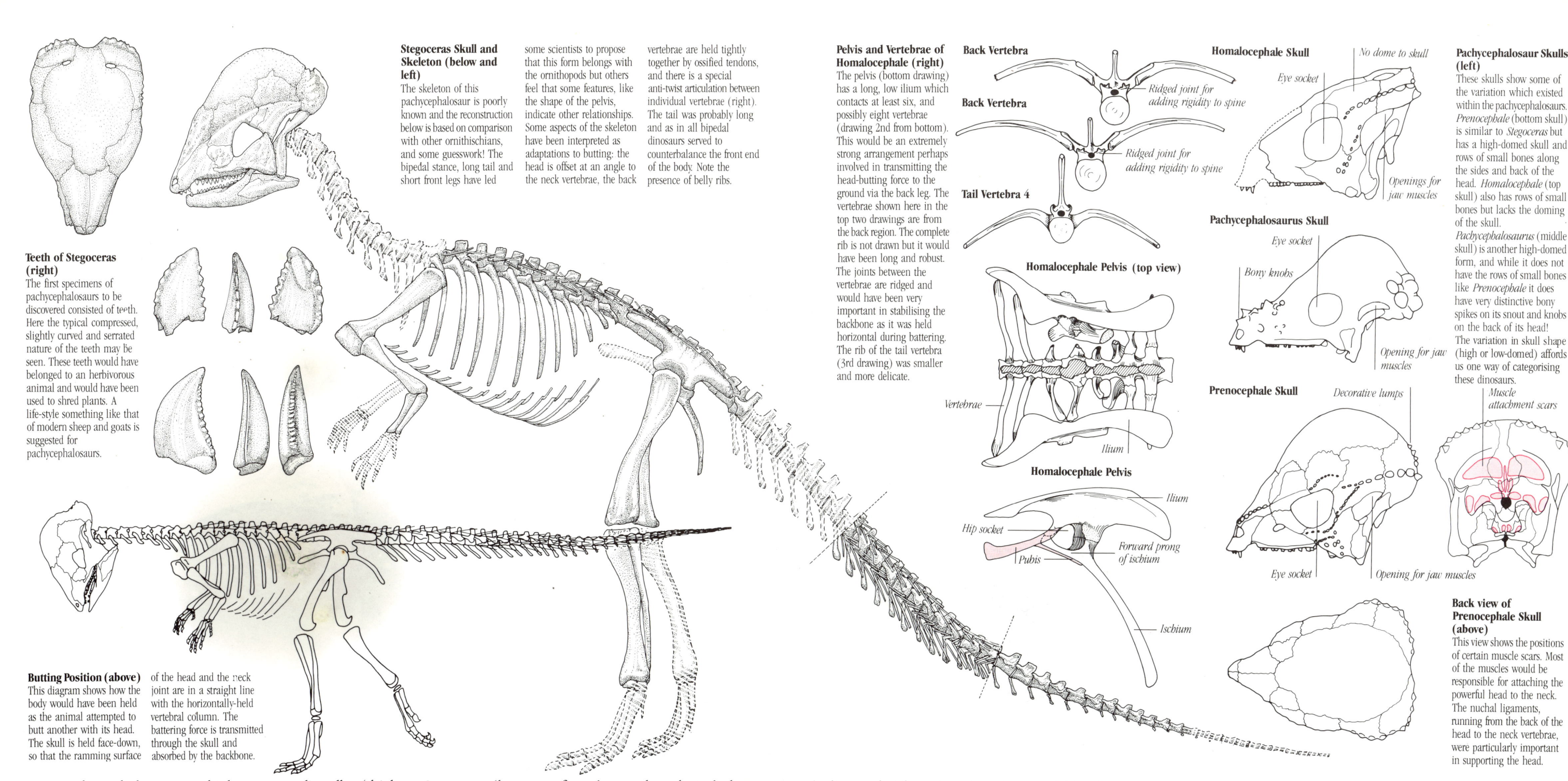

Stegoceras Skull and Skeleton (below and left)
The skeleton of this pachycephalosaur is poorly known and the reconstruction below is based on comparison with other ornithischians, and some guesswork! The bipedal stance, long tail and short front legs have led some scientists to propose that this form belongs with the ornithopods but others feel that some features, like the shape of the pelvis, indicate other relationships. Some aspects of the skeleton have been interpreted as adaptations to butting: the head is offset at an angle to the neck vertebrae, the back vertebrae are held tightly together by ossified tendons, and there is a special anti-twist articulation between individual vertebrae (right). The tail was probably long and as in all bipedal dinosaurs served to counterbalance the front end of the body. Note the presence of belly ribs.

Teeth of Stegoceras (right)
The first specimens of pachycephalosaurs to be discovered consisted of teeth. Here the typical compressed, slightly curved and serrated nature of the teeth may be seen. These teeth would have belonged to an herbivorous animal and would have been used to shred plants. A life-style something like that of modern sheep and goats is suggested for pachycephalosaurs.

Butting Position (above)
This diagram shows how the body would have been held as the animal attempted to butt another with its head. The skull is held face-down, so that the ramming surface of the head and the neck joint are in a straight line with the horizontally-held vertebral column. The battering force is transmitted through the skull and absorbed by the backbone.

Pelvis and Vertebrae of Homalocephale (right)
The pelvis (bottom drawing) has a long, low ilium which contacts at least six, and possibly eight vertebrae (drawing 2nd from bottom). This would be an extremely strong arrangement perhaps involved in transmitting the head-butting force to the ground via the back leg. The vertebrae shown here in the top two drawings are from the back region. The complete rib is not drawn but it would have been long and robust. The joints between the vertebrae are ridged and would have been very important in stabilising the backbone as it was held horizontal during battering. The rib of the tail vertebra (3rd drawing) was smaller and more delicate.

Back Vertebra — *Ridged joint for adding rigidity to spine*
Back Vertebra — *Ridged joint for adding rigidity to spine*
Tail Vertebra 4
Homalocephale Pelvis (top view)
Vertebrae
Ilium
Homalocephale Pelvis
Hip socket — *Pubis* — *Ilium* — *Forward prong of ischium* — *Ischium*

Homalocephale Skull
Eye socket — *No dome to skull* — *Openings for jaw muscles*

Pachycephalosaurus Skull
Eye socket — *Bony knobs* — *Opening for jaw muscles*

Prenocephale Skull
Decorative lumps — *Muscle attachment scars* — *Eye socket* — *Opening for jaw muscles*

Pachycephalosaur Skulls (left)
These skulls show some of the variation which existed within the pachycephalosaurs. *Prenocephale* (bottom skull) is similar to *Stegoceras* but has a high-domed skull and rows of small bones along the sides and back of the head. *Homalocephale* (top skull) also has rows of small bones but lacks the doming of the skull. *Pachycephalosaurus* (middle skull) is another high-domed form, and while it does not have the rows of small bones like *Prenocephale* it does have very distinctive bony spikes on its snout and knobs on the back of its head! The variation in skull shape (high or low-domed) affords us one way of categorising these dinosaurs.

Back view of Prenocephale Skull (above)
This view shows the positions of certain muscle scars. Most of the muscles would have been responsible for attaching the powerful head to the neck. The nuchal ligaments, running from the back of the head to the neck vertebrae, were particularly important in supporting the head.

Pachycephalosaurs, which means literally 'thick headed reptiles' are a quite rare group of very strange looking dinosaurs that lived toward the end of the Cretaceous Period. The early history of the discovery of these dinosaurs is rather confusing because they are extremely rare and the pieces that are found are often broken and difficult to recognise.

Many years ago, during the 1850s, when the rocks of North America were only just being surveyed for the first time, several pieces of fossil were collected. Some teeth, like the ones seen above, were found in Montana and were given to name *Troodon* (wounding tooth). More teeth of this type were later found in Canada. At about the same time that the second lot of teeth were found in Canada (1902), a few broken pieces of head were also discovered. The pieces of head were unusually thick and were named *Stegoceras* (horny roof) and were thought to belong to a ceratopid dinosaur. A little later a few more fragments were found and it was then thought that the animal may have been a stegosaurid (see pages 42-43). And so things went on until in 1924 (70 years after the first teeth were found) when a complete head and part of a skeleton were discovered in Alberta. The animal was described as *Troodon* because its teeth seemed to be like those teeth found in the 1850s even though the head was just like those pieces that were named *Stegoceras*! Confused? So you should be. It is an example of the sorts of tangles that scientists can get into when they are trying to work with very incomplete fossils.

What is now decided is that the animal found in Alberta should be called *Stegoceras*, because teeth alone are not very good indicators of exactly what sort of animal you are dealing with. The original teeth named *Troodon* are now thought to belong to a small meat eating dinosaur, something like the coelurosaurs on pages 6-7.

Stegoceras is a fairly small dinosaur about 2m (6ft) long and has the shape of an ornithopod dinosaur something like the *Hypsilophodon* (page 26). It ran on its back legs and had a long stiff tail and quite small front legs and hands. Its head was the most peculiar thing about this dinosaur because it was capped by the most enormous thickness of solid bone.

Pachycephalosaurus (thick-headed reptile) gave its name to this group of dinosaurs since it is the largest member of the group. To date only its skull has been discovered. It comes from Montana and is very impressive being nearly 1m (3ft) long and extremely heavy. The animal must have been somewhere in the region of 8-9m (25-30ft) in length.

Homalocephale (even head) was discovered much more recently in Mongolia, and is a rather unusual pachycephalosaur in that it does not have a very thick head. The head is quite strong and obviously built like that of other pachycephalosaurs, but it does not have the dome of bone on top. The nice thing about the discovery of this animal is that it also has quite a good skeleton, which tells us a good deal more about how these animals may have lived.

Prenocephale (sloping head) is another new find from Mongolia and looks quite a lot like *Stegoceras*. The very thick bone on the head and the stiffening seen in the back and tail of these animals suggests that they used their heads for butting. This is the sort of thing that sheep and goats do today and it is very tempting to see pachycephalosaurs as the dinosaur versions of these animals, perhaps living in small groups in upland areas.

STEGOSAURIDS
Clockwise from top left: Tuojiangosaurus, Stegosaurus, Kentrosaurus

Stegosaurus Skeleton and Body Sections (centre)

This genus shows basic stegosaurid features well: the relatively small head, the short front legs compared with the back ones, the large bony plates along the back, and the tail spines. You can see clearly the variation in shape of the plates along the body, and by looking at the sections through the body at certain points along the animal (drawings at foot of page) you can see how the angle of attachment of the plates varies — it is very wide in the lower tail region. The tail spikes were used for defence, being swung from side to side by powerful tail muscles. The marked difference in length of fore and hindlimbs is readily apparent.

Kentrosaurus Skeleton (below)

The front plates of both *Kentrosaurus* and *Stegosaurus* are similar in shape, but over the hip region and down the tail they become compressed into long, narrow spikes in *Kentrosaurus* which also has an extra spike pointing down and outwards from the hip.

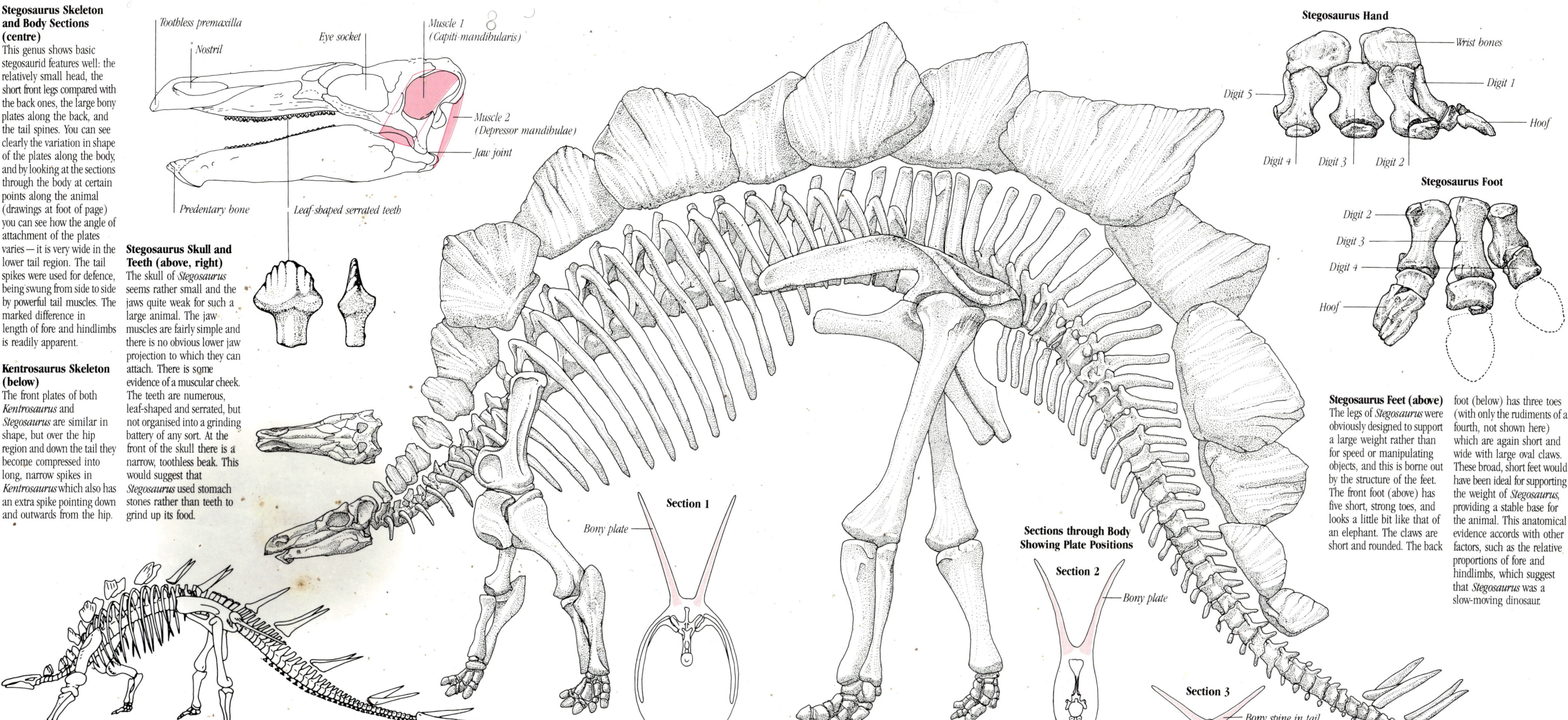

Stegosaurus Skull and Teeth (above, right)

The skull of *Stegosaurus* seems rather small and the jaws quite weak for such a large animal. The jaw muscles are fairly simple and there is no obvious lower jaw projection to which they can attach. There is some evidence of a muscular cheek. The teeth are numerous, leaf-shaped and serrated, but not organised into a grinding battery of any sort. At the front of the skull there is a narrow, toothless beak. This would suggest that *Stegosaurus* used stomach stones rather than teeth to grind up its food.

Stegosaurus Feet (above)

The legs of *Stegosaurus* were obviously designed to support a large weight rather than for speed or manipulating objects, and this is borne out by the structure of the feet. The front foot (above) has five short, strong toes, and looks a little bit like that of an elephant. The claws are short and rounded. The back foot (below) has three toes (with only the rudiments of a fourth, not shown here) which are again short and wide with large oval claws. These broad, short feet would have been ideal for supporting the weight of *Stegosaurus*, providing a stable base for the animal. This anatomical evidence accords with other factors, such as the relative proportions of fore and hindlimbs, which suggest that *Stegosaurus* was a slow-moving dinosaur.

Stegosaurids are a group of quite large four-footed dinosaurs, which are very distinctive because they have rows of big bony plates or spines that run down their backs. Relatively few stegosaurids have been discovered, but *Stegosaurus* from Colorado, Wyoming and Utah in the USA is one of the best known of all dinosaurs. Almost all the fossils of stegosaurids come from the late Jurassic Period and they have been found in Africa, Europe, India and China as well as in North America.

The first remains of stegosaurids went largely unrecognised at the time. They were first found in Britain in the early 1870s but, even though these remains included the large and distinctive plates of bone that run down the back, the discoveries were largely ignored because in the late 1870s some fabulous skeletons of the real *Stegosaurus* were discovered in western North America.

Stegosaurus (roofed reptile) was a moderate size by dinosaur standards. The largest skeletons that are known are about 8m (25ft) long. The body of the dinosaur is slightly unusual because the back legs are very long and pillar-like to support the main weight of the body, while the front legs are strong, but very short, so that the body slopes down from a high rump toward the head. The advantage of this arrangement is that it brings the head very close to the ground so that the animal does not have to stoop down to feed like some of the taller dinosaurs may have had to.

The head of the *Stegosaurus* is very small for the size of the animal and is rather long and thin. It is possible that the head was this shape so that it could feed on a special sort of plant, but this is just a guess. For defence against the big meat eaters of the time such as *Allosaurus* (see pages 12-13) it could not have used its head, for there were no large teeth or horns to use as weapons. Instead it used a sting in its tail! The end of its tail had pairs of long — up to 1m (3ft) — spikes sticking up in the air. These could be lashed from side to side against their attackers when they came close enough, causing horrible injuries.

It had been thought for a long time that the big plates of bone running down the spine were also a part of their defence system, forming an armour plating against claws and teeth. Some work has recently shown that these plates are nothing to do with defence, but had a lot to do with keeping the body at the correct temperature. It seems that they were filled with blood which ran underneath the skin and could be either warmed by the sun or cooled in a breeze so that the dinosaur could keep itself at just the right temperature during the day rather like the water in central heating system of a house.

Kentrosaurus (prickly reptile) comes from the late Jurassic of Tanzania in Africa and was found near the remains of the gigantic sauropod *Brachiosaurus* (pages 20-21). Smaller than *Stegosaurus*, measuring about 2.5m (8ft) long, it was a much more prickly reptile than *Stegosaurus* as its name suggests. The sharp spikes that are only found at the end of the tail in *Stegosaurus* spread right up the length of the tail and across the hips. In fact there are even an extra pair of spines that stick out from the sides of the hip bones as you will see if you look carefully at the pictures. These spines were primarily to deter predators.

Tuojiangosaurus (reptile of Tuojiang) is a 6m (20ft) long Chinese stegosaur, which also comes from the late Jurassic and has rather narrow plates than run down the length of its back and large spikes on its tail. It almost seems like a cross between *Stegosaurus* and *Kentrosaurus*.

NODOSAURIDS

Clockwise from top: Nodosaurus, Polacanthus, Hylaeosaurus

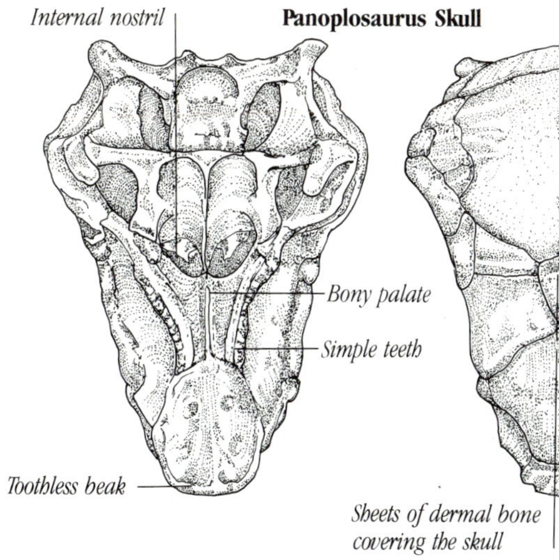

Internal nostril **Panoplosaurus Skull**

Bony palate
Simple teeth
Toothless beak
Sheets of dermal bone covering the skull

Panoplosaurus Skull (above)
From above (right) the details of the armour plating are clear; the grooves show where the slabs of bone join. From below one can see the toothless beak on the snout, the teeth, the internal nostrils and the braincase behind.

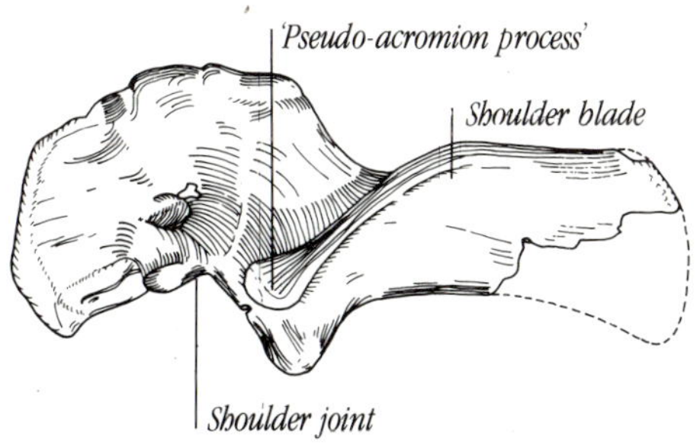

'Pseudo-acromion process'
Shoulder blade
Shoulder joint

Nodosaur Shoulder Blade (left)
This shoulder blade belongs to *Sauropelta* and is typical of the type seen in nodosaurids. Its most outstanding feature, and one in which it differs from that of ankylosaurids, is the large pseudo-acromion process which overhangs the shoulder joint and which may have improved the mechanical advantage of some of the shoulder muscles. It is possible that this allowed nodosaurids to crouch against the ground for protection against predators, relying on their armour to withstand any attack.

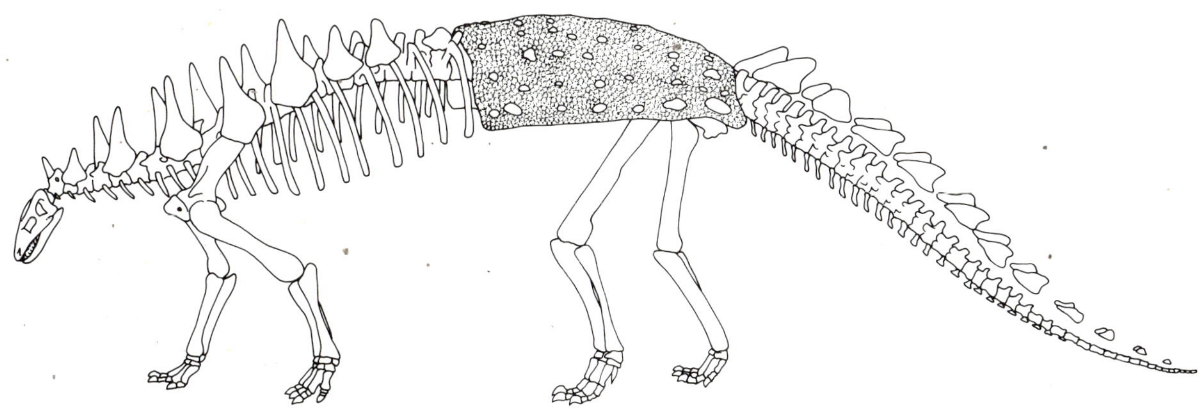

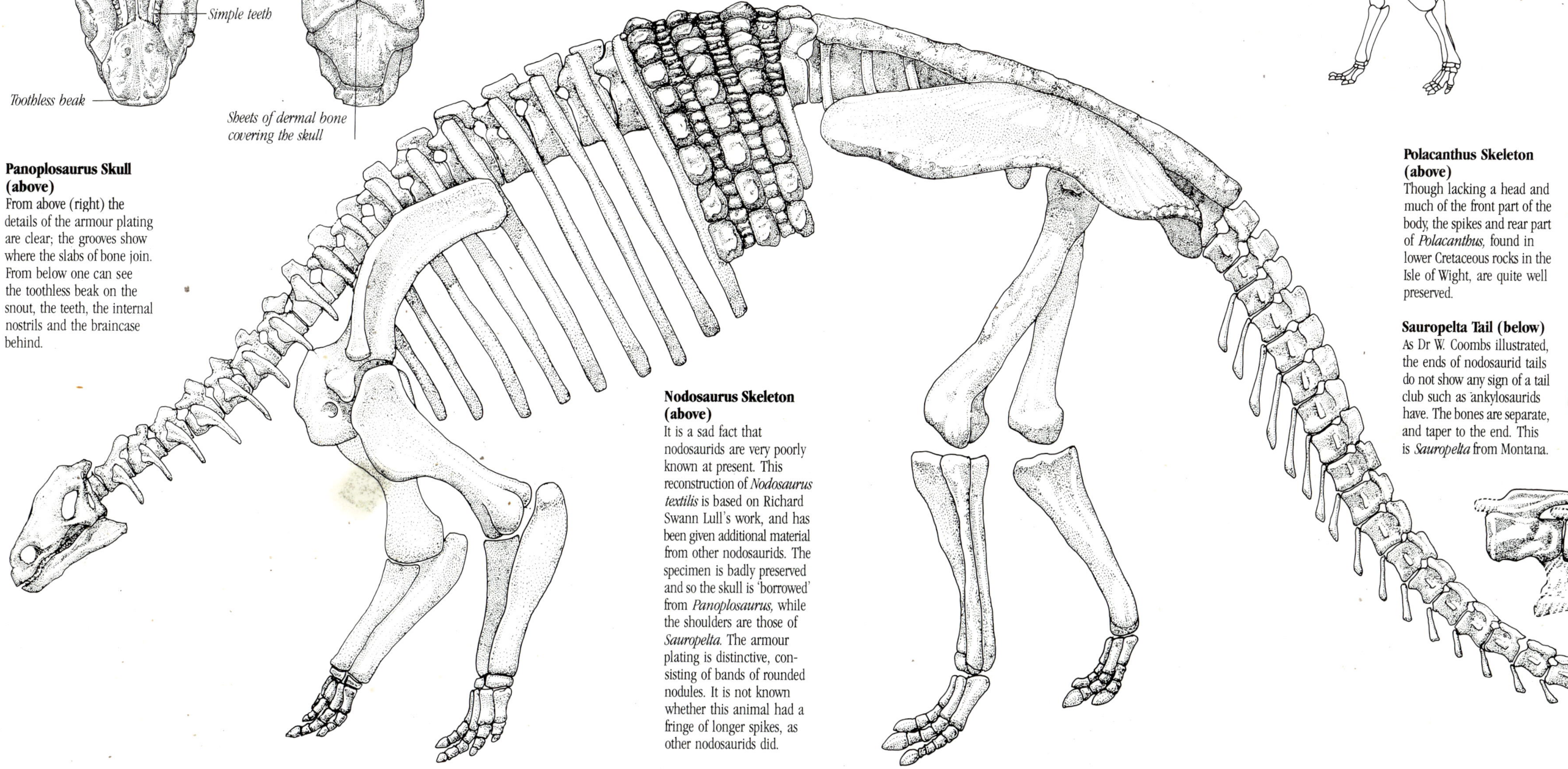

Nodosaurus Skeleton (above)
It is a sad fact that nodosaurids are very poorly known at present. This reconstruction of *Nodosaurus textilis* is based on Richard Swann Lull's work, and has been given additional material from other nodosaurids. The specimen is badly preserved and so the skull is 'borrowed' from *Panoplosaurus*, while the shoulders are those of *Sauropelta*. The armour plating is distinctive, consisting of bands of rounded nodules. It is not known whether this animal had a fringe of longer spikes, as other nodosaurids did.

Polacanthus Skeleton (above)
Though lacking a head and much of the front part of the body, the spikes and rear part of *Polacanthus*, found in lower Cretaceous rocks in the Isle of Wight, are quite well preserved.

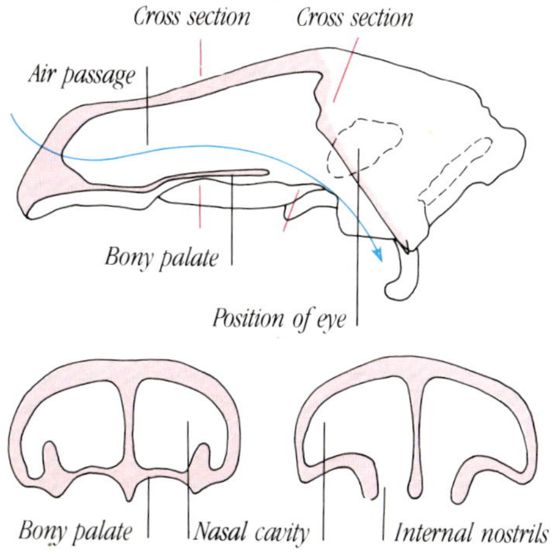

Sauropelta Tail (below)
As Dr W. Coombs illustrated, the ends of nodosaurid tails do not show any sign of a tail club such as ankylosaurids have. The bones are separate, and taper to the end. This is *Sauropelta* from Montana.

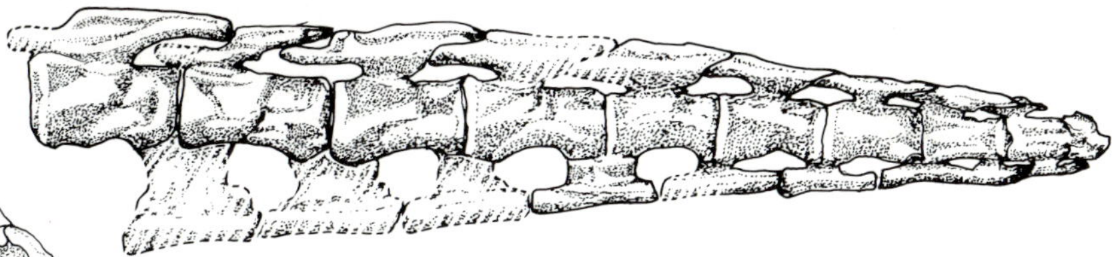

Cross section *Cross section*
Air passage
Bony palate
Position of eye
Bony palate *Nasal cavity* *Internal nostrils*

Panoplosaurus Skull Sections (left)
Above right the skull is seen in longitudinal section to show the air passage from the outer nostril to the inner nostril at the back of the throat. A hard bony palate separates the mouth and nasal cavities. This may have allowed these animals to breathe while chewing. This is also found in ankylosaurids. The lower cross sections taken near the front (left) and rear of the snout show the extent of the bony palate and nasal passages.

The last of the major groups of ornithischian dinosaur to be looked at are the ankylosaurs. For simplicity the ankylosaurs have been divided into two groups; the nodosaurids and the ankylosaurids (pages 46-47). These groups can be easily distinguished because ankylosaurids have a very large bony tail club, while nodosaurids have a normal tail.

Ankylosaurs are known from Jurassic and Cretaceous rocks in North America, Europe, Asia and Australia. The unusual name ankylosaur, which means 'joined or fused reptiles', refers to the fact that the skin of these animals has bones in it. In some cases the pieces of bone have become welded (fused) together into great pieces of shield-like armour. These bones are sometimes welded on to the head giving the creature a grotesque appearance. The armour plating was no doubt for their defence against some of the large meat eating dinosaurs that lived at the same time, and made these ankylosaurs into the armoured tanks of the dinosaur world. They are all about about 4m (13ft) long.

Nodosaurids include the first ever discovered ankylosaurs. The very first to be found and described was *Hylaeosaurus*, which comes from south-east Britain.

Hylaeosaurus (forest reptile) was found in a stone quarry in Tilgate Forest (hence the name) in 1833. The skeleton, which was discovered by Dr. Gideon Mantell, was unfortunately not complete; it consisted of the front half of a dinosaur embedded in a large block of limestone. Unfortunately, this fossil, which is now in the British Museum, is still embedded in the limestone block, so we cannot be entirely sure what it looked like in life. However, the exposed parts indicate that the back of *Hylaeosaurus* had a row of large curved spines sticking out.

Polacanthus (many-spined) is another British nodosaurid which is, again, not at all well preserved and is therefore difficult to make an accurate picture of. By contrast to *Hylaeosaurus*, the remains of *Polacanthus* found on the Isle of Wight, which lies just off the southern coast of Britain, consist of the rear half of the skeleton. Included are the back legs, hips and much of the tail with its bony armour, and some of the armour from the chest. Both *Hylaeosaurus* and *Polacanthus* come from the early Cretaceous Period and it has been proposed by some scientists that they are one and the same beast, but until either *Hylaeosaurus* is cleared of the stone that surrounds its skeleton or better preserved material is found we cannot be sure.

Nodosaurus (lumpy reptile) comes from the late Cretaceous Period of Kansas and Wyoming and even though it seems to be quite well preserved in the illustration above, it is not really. Most of its bones are in very bad shape, and to make this picture up we have had to cheat by using spare parts from other nodosaurids.

Panoplosaurus (fully-plated reptile) is known from a well preserved skull. It is, in fact, used as the model for the skull on the *Nodosaurus* skeleton, as well as in the detailed drawings. The top of the head is covered in large plates of bone, which would have made it enormously strong.

Sauropelta (shielded reptile) is the only other moderately well known nodosaurid. It comes from the middle Cretaceous of Montana. Living at the same time and in the same area as *Deinonychus* (pages 10-11) was undoubtedly a good reason for being heavily armoured.

As a defence against attack, nodosaurids simply relied on their armoured skin, but as we shall see the ankylosaurids were much better equipped.

ANKYLOSAURIDS
Pinacosaurus (top) and Euoplocephalus

Euoplocepalus Skull
Top View

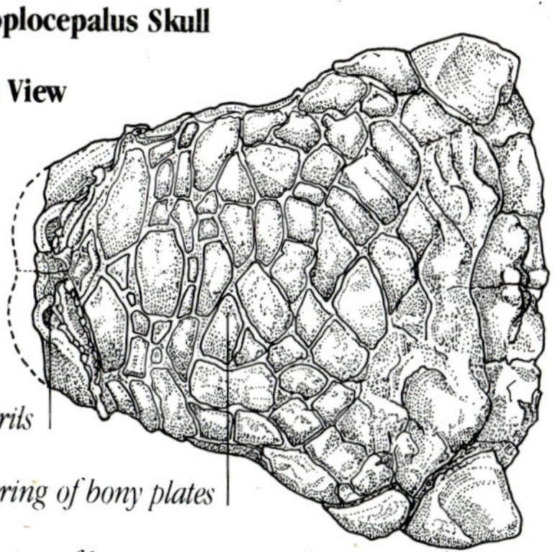

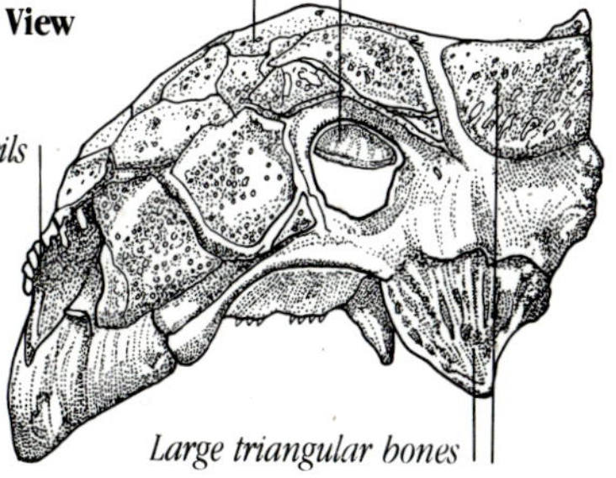

Nostrils
Covering of bony plates
Covering of bony plates
Bony eyelid

Side View

Nostrils
Large triangular bones

View Up Into Palate

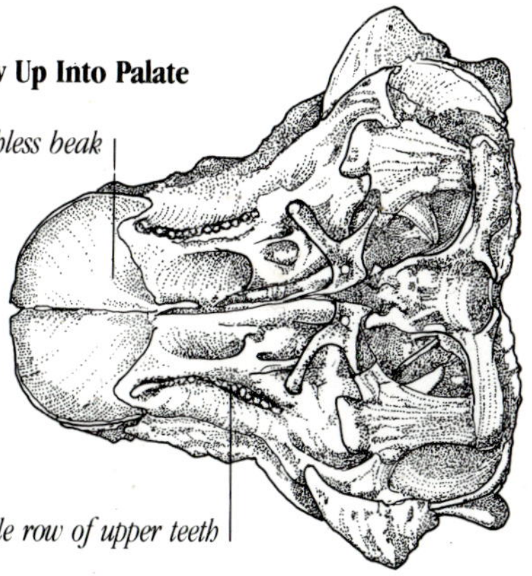

Toothless beak
Feeble row of upper teeth

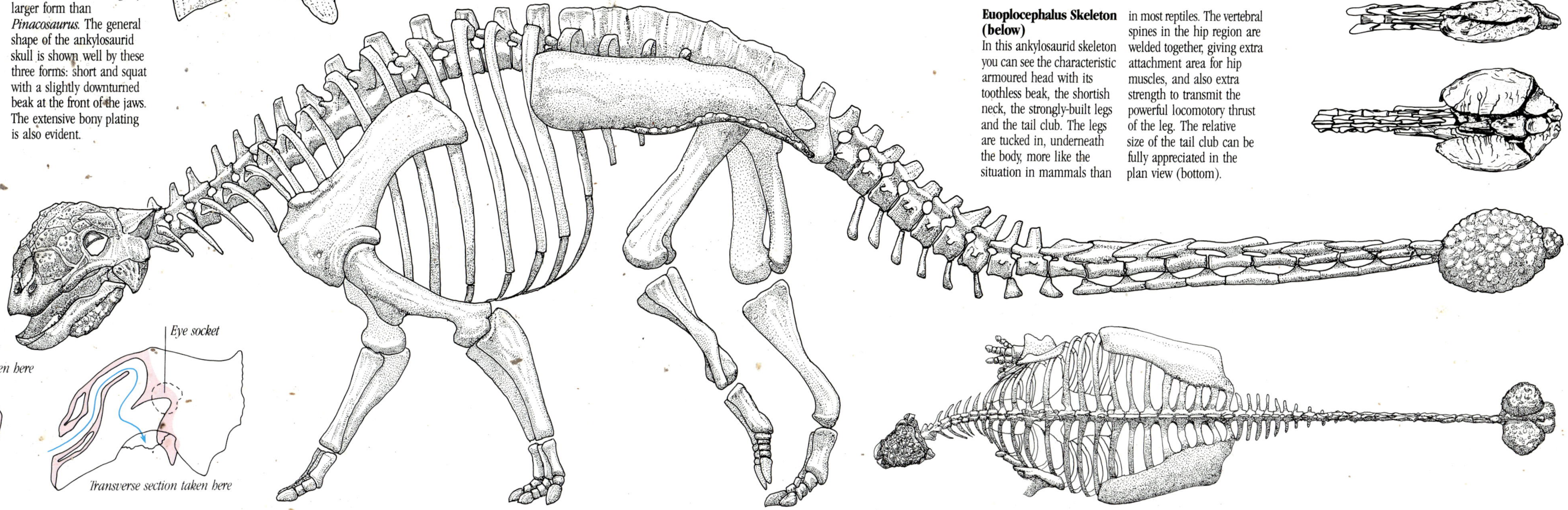

Sectioned Skull of Euoplocephalus (right)
The first drawing shows the skull cut through parallel to its back surface. Note the numerous sinuses. The next drawing shows the skull cut at 90° to the first cut. (Red shows respiratory passages).

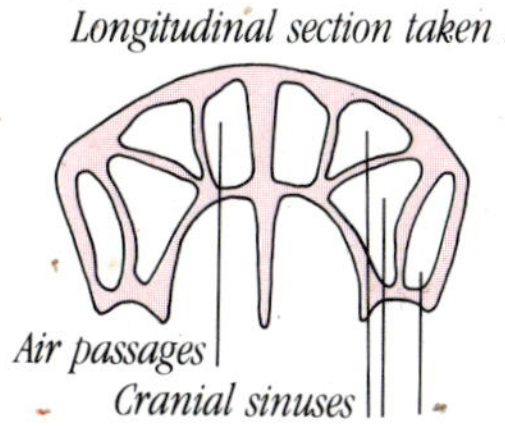

Longitudinal section taken here
Eye socket
Air passages
Cranial sinuses
Transverse section taken here

Ankylosaurid Skulls (left, right)
The skulls here show basic ankylosaurid features: they are about as broad as they are long; they are armoured, with the sides completely closed in; and they have large horns at the back corners. *Euoplocephalus* (three drawings at left) is remarkable since it even has bony eyelids! Notice how compact and immensely strong the skull looks. The skull of *Pinacosaurus* shown here (immediately right) is a juvenile and the individual bones of the skull can still be seen — in adults they are welded together. The skull of *Saichania* (two drawings far right) is more knobbly than the others. It was a slightly larger form than *Pinacosaurus*. The general shape of the ankylosaurid skull is shown well by these three forms: short and squat with a slightly downturned beak at the front of the jaws. The extensive bony plating is also evident.

Pinacosaurus Skull
Top View

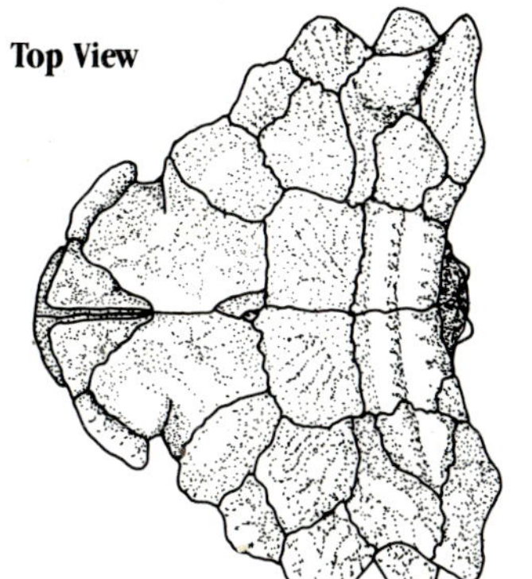

Side View

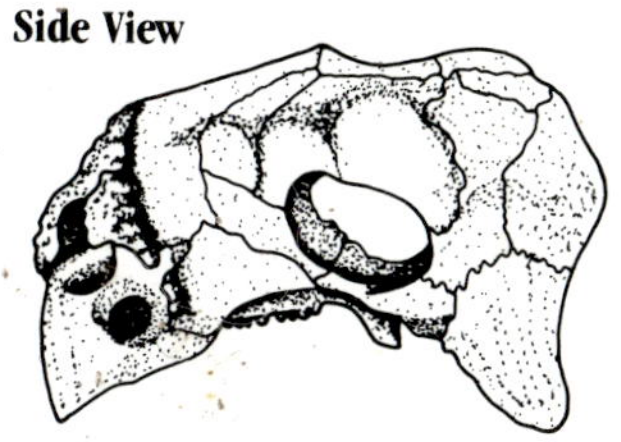

Saichania Skull
Top View

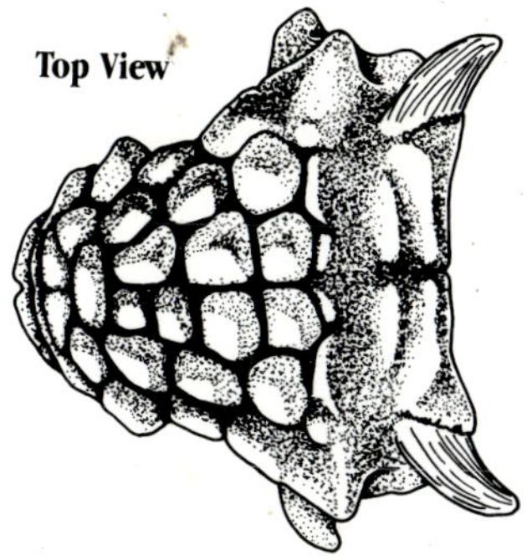

Side View

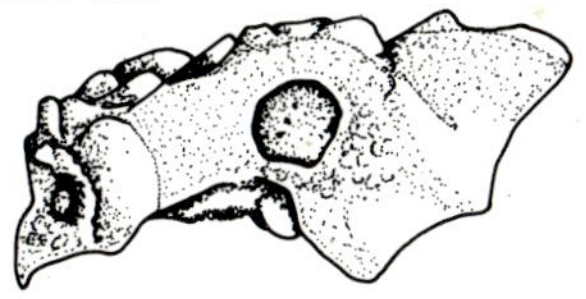

Shoulder and Hip Muscles (right)
Although the muscles are labelled here with just one function, this is merely their primary function. Usually muscles exert quite a complex force. For example, the coracobrachialis pulls forwards, but also inwards and upwards. Ankylosaurids needed powerful leg muscles to support and move their rather large, heavy bodies. Notice the bulky muscles arising from the back of the hip region. In most reptiles these pull the leg back, but here they are also responsible for swinging the tail, a very important part of the ankylosaurid defensive armoury.

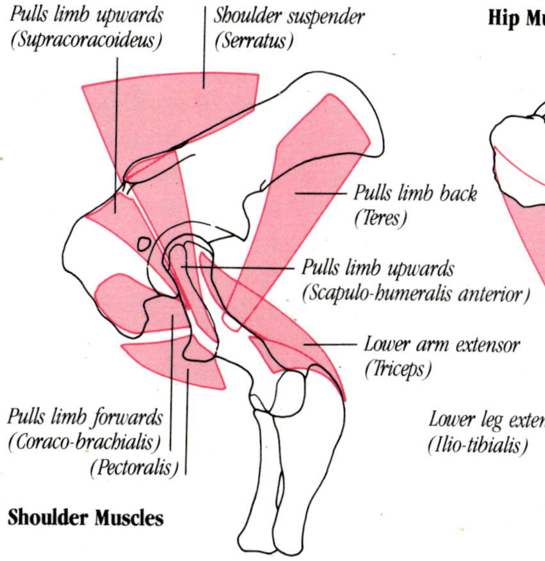

Shoulder Muscles

Pulls limb upwards (Supracoracoideus)
Shoulder suspender (Serratus)
Pulls limb back (Teres)
Pulls limb upwards (Scapulo-humeralis anterior)
Lower arm extensor (Triceps)
Pulls limb forwards (Coraco-brachialis) (Pectoralis)

Hip Muscles

Club-swinging muscles (Ilio-caudalis) (Caudi-femoralis longus)
Lower leg flexors (Flexor tibialis anterior) (Ilio-fibularis)
Lower leg extensors (Ilio-tibialis)

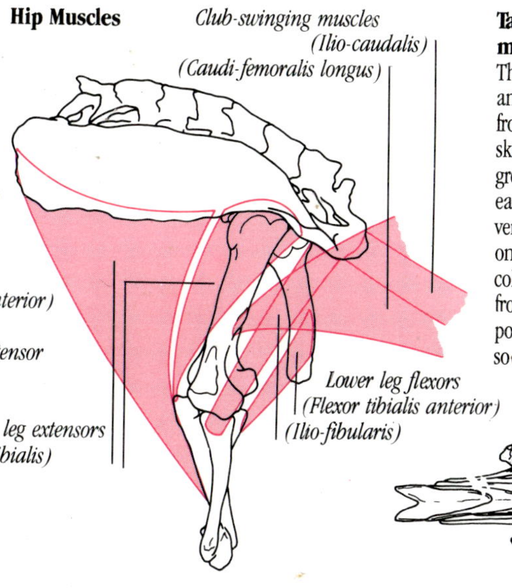

Tail of Ankylosaurus magniventris (below)
The tail club is unique to ankylosaurids. It is formed from bones embedded in the skin which have become greatly enlarged and fused to each other and to the tail vertebrae. It forms two lobes, one each side of the vertebral column, and could be swung from side to side by the powerful tail muscles, and so used as a weapon.

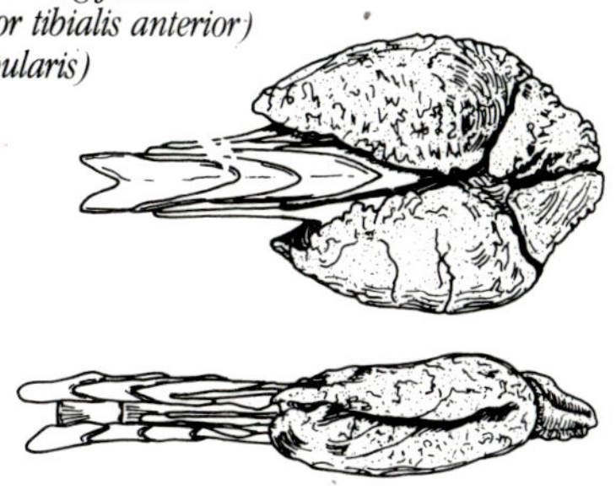

Euoplocephalus Skeleton (below)
In this ankylosaurid skeleton you can see the characteristic armoured head with its toothless beak, the shortish neck, the strongly-built legs and the tail club. The legs are tucked in, underneath the body, more like the situation in mammals than in most reptiles. The vertebral spines in the hip region are welded together, giving extra attachment area for hip muscles, and also extra strength to transmit the powerful locomotory thrust of the leg. The relative size of the tail club can be fully appreciated in the plan view (bottom).

In addition to the tail club, there are a number of other differences between ankylosaurids and nodosaurid ankylosaurs. Ankylosaurids have much broader heads which tend to be pointed at the back corners and the sides of the skull are more heavily armoured. The armour plates that cover the body are also much less spiky than those of nodosaurids. In addition, ankylosaurids seem only to be found in the Cretaceous Period and to be confined to two areas in the world: North America and Asia.

Euoplocephalus (true plated head), one of the best known of the North American ankylosaurids, was a large and heavily built animal. It grew to a length of at least 6m (20ft) and has been found in rocks that date from near the end of the Cretaceous Period.

The first remains of this animal, consisting of the head and part of the body, were recovered from the Red Deer River of Alberta in the early 1900s. Since that time quite a lot more material of this dinosaur, as well as other armoured dinosaurs, has been recovered from this area.

As illustrated, the animal has large and powerful legs, which would have been necessary to support the enormous weight of its armour-plating. Unlike the ceratopids and stegosaurs, the front legs are not particularly short. Not shown here, but found in the fossils of these dinosaurs, are the thin bony rods that strengthen the backbone and helped to support the weight of these animals; these bony rods do not form the very obvious structures that we saw in some of the larger ornithopods (pages 30-33), but are found in bundles around the end of the tail close to the bony tail club. The reason for this arrangement is to help the tail bones to resist whip-lash damage when the tail club was being used.

In the case of heavy and powerful dinosaurs, it is possible to work out how the muscles of the legs functioned. What is needed are some well preserved leg, hip and shoulder bones, which have, indeed, been found in the case of the *Euoplocephalus*. It is possible to see the areas where the muscles were attached to the bones because they leave clear marks, or scars, on the bone surface. Using these scars the muscles can be drawn in, as you will see in the diagrams above.

The extent to which these dinosaurs were armour-plated is surprising. No only is the bone around the head very thick, with slabs of bone plastered all over the top, it is also found on the eyelid! Small, curved bones which must have been eyelids, have been found in the eye socket of one of the skulls of *Euoplocephalus*. These would have prevented meat eating dinosaurs from clawing their eyes out.

Pinacosaurus (plank reptile) comes from Mongolia and is known from quite a lot of material. It was more lightly built and smaller—5m (16ft) long—than *Euoplocephalus*. Quite recently, more material has been discovered in Mongolia which includes the skull of a young one. In this very rare fossil it is possible to see the way in which the bones on the skull gradually grow over and become welded together, forming a solid sheet.

Saichania (beautiful) also from Mongolia is known from the front half of a skeleton. It grew a little larger at 7m (23ft) and has a particularly knobbly sort of head.

With its large bony club, the tail of the ankylosaurids was undoubtedly used as a defensive weapon and would have been swung against the legs of an attacker; this would have been a very effective way of disabling a two-legged tyrannosaurid.

GLOSSARY

A

Abductor
Closer (i.e. jaw adductor muscle is a jaw-closing example into the Classes *Mammalia* and *Aves* (birds).

Amphibia, Reptilia,
Dale Russell's name for his imaginative reconstruction of how the theropod dinosaur *Stenonychosaurus* might have evolved if it had not gone extinct 64 million years ago.

Algae
Aquatic plants, both small and large.

Anapsid
A reptile group including the living turtles and tortoises characterised by having no skull openings behind the eye socket.

Archosaurs
A major group of reptiles which includes the dinosaurs, pterosaurs, thecodontians — all of which are extinct — and the living crocodiles.

Arthropods
Animals with jointed legs, e.g. insects, spiders, crabs

Articulated
Joined together by jointed braincase.

B

Biped
An habitually two-footed dinosaurs about 64 million years ago.

Browsers
Those animals that feed on high foliage (shrubs and trees).

C

Cambrian Period
The most ancient of the Palaeozoic time zones, rocks of this period show the first traces of fairly complicated animal life.

Cantilever
A beam or lever that projects outward from its support for example, it makes and complicated animal life.

Carapace
A hard outer covering to the body, such as the shell of a tortoise.

Chevrons
Bones hanging below the tail.

Class
Below the level of *Phylum*, (see below). The term is from the Greek meaning 'rank' or 'fearfully great reptile'.

Classification
The process of ordering or classifying organisms into groups which are related by descent.

Clavicle
Collar bone.

Conifers
Cone-bearing trees such as firs, pines and yews.

Continental Drift
The phenomenon of continental movement (Drift) on tectonic plates in the Earth's crust.

Coronoid process
From above (opposite of lower jaw for the attachment of jaw-closing muscles.

Cranial
Relating to the cranium or braincase.

Cretaceous Period
The third Period in the Mesozoic Era, it lasted from 135 million years ago until chemical reactions in order to regulate the body temperature.

Cycads
Squat, rather palm-tree-like shelled sea creatures that look a little like clams and oysters but are not closely related.

D

Deposit (geological)
Accumulation of rock.

Dermal bone
Bone formed within the skin.

Diapsid
A reptile group, including the dinosaurs, lizards, snakes and their descendants the birds, characterised by having a pair of openings immediately behind the eye socket.

Dinosaur
A special type of land-living reptile with an erect gait — a member of the archosaur group — that flourished between 225 and 64 million years ago.

Dimorphism
The characteristic of having two forms — usually sexual. For example, it is males and females of the same species look different, then the species is said to exhibit sexual dimorphism.

Dispersal
The process of spreading out, in a geographic sense.

Divergence
The process of something that once lived, it can be formed in a number of ways, usually involving burial with structured, fish-shaped vertebrae.

Dorsal
From above (opposite of ventral).

E

Endothermic — being 'Warm-blooded' — being able to generate heat internally by means of

F

Fauna
Animals of similar genera look different, then the species is said to exhibit sexual dimorphism.

Femur
Upper leg or thigh-bone.

Fenestra
Window-like opening in the skull.

Fibula
Shin bone (see also *tibia*).

Flexor muscle
A muscle which bends a joint, as opposed to an extensor which straightens a joint.

Flora
Plants.

Foliage
Leaves, branches and twigs.

Forelimbs
Front pair of arms/wings.

Fossil
The notion that those Marine reptiles of the Mesozoic Era, these were the most highly specialised adapted for swimming.

Fossilisation
The process by which a fossil is the preserved evidence of fossils.

I

Ichthyosaurs
Marine reptiles of the Mesozoic Era, these were the most highly specialised adapted for swimming.

Illium
One of the bones of the pelvis, it is connected to the backbone.

Insectivores
Insect-eaters.

Iridium
A heavy metal element found in meteorites and the Earth's core.

Ischium
One of the pelvic bones; it provides a socket (on the underside) for the backward projection of the hip socket.

G

Gait
Characteristics of movement.

Gastralia
Belly ribs.

Gastroliths
'Stomach stones', used either for ballast or for pounding up food or as a

Genealogy
The result of weathering in jaw in ornithischian dinosaurs alone.

Geographical distribution
A gradual change in a population of organisms over generations — the basic characteristics of a natural selection.

Geological timescale
Relating to the history of the Earth — based on a characteristics of a natural selection.

Geologist
A person who studies the origin and nature of the weather.

Geology
The science of the study of the Earth's rocks.

Ginkgo
The maidenhair tree of East Asia, is the sole survivor of a once abundant group of gymnosperm trees.

Grazers
Those animals that feed on grasses (and other low-lying vegetation).

H

Hadrosaurine
Non-crested hadrosaurid.

Humerus
Upper arm bone.

Hyperextended
Over-straightened; bent backwards on itself.

L

Lambeosaurine
Relating to hadrosaurids with large tubular crests on skull.

Ligaments
Tough sheets or threads of protein (collagen) which support joints between bones.

M

Mantle
A region of the Earth's interior between the outer and the core.

Mesozoic
'Middle life'. The period of time (Era, between 225-64 million years ago comprising the Triassic, Jurassic and Cretaceous Periods.

Metacarpals
Long bones in the upper part of the hand that form the palm.

Metatarsals
Back of rear legs.

N

Natural selection
The notion that those organisms that are best adapted for prevailing conditions will survive to perpetuate their kind i.e. the environment 'selects', the fittest organisms. A quintessential part of Charles Darwin's Theory of Evolution.

Neural spine
A spine rising above a vertebra and protecting the spinal cord.

Nuchal ligaments
Neck ligaments (from Latin *ligamentum nuchae*).

O

Omnivore
An animal with a diet of both plant and animal food.

Order
A category of animals that includes a variety of similar families.

Ornithischian
One of the two major Orders of dinosaurs (see also *saurischian*) which is based on hip structure, in ornithischians the pubis is parallel to the ischium (as in birds). The group is entirely herbivorous and includes ornithopods, stegosaurs and ankylosaurs.

P

Palaeontologist
A person who studies fossils.

Palaeontology
The study of fossils.

Palaeozoic
'Ancient life'. The period of time (Era, between 600-225 million years ago) comprising the Cambrian, Ordovician, Silurian, Devonian, Carboniferous and Permian periods.

Palpebral
Small bone found in the rim of the eye socket, especially by the arrival of Man, 1.8 million years ago to the present day.

Para-sacral spines
Bony spikes, projecting from the hip region in stegosaurs.

Pelvis

Long bones in the upper part of the foot.

Permineralisation
Deposition of minerals inside a bony fossil.

Petrification
'Turning to stone'; the replacement, by minerals, of the original hard tissues in fossilised organisms, so that it becomes stone-like in nature.

Plesiosaurs
A bone found at the tip of the snout (maxilla) in ceratopian dinosaurs only.

Pleurocoel
A cavity in the sides of vertebrae.

Q

Quadruped
An habitually four-footed creature.

Quaternary Period
The recent prehistoric past (see above) from the arrival of Man, 1.8 million years ago to the present day.

R

Radius
One of the two forearm bones (see also *ulna*).

Recurved
Curved backwards (of teeth).

S

Sacral ribs
Special strong ribs that connect the vertebral column to the pelvis.

Sacrum
Referring to the vast Period of time (before the Cambrian Period) that elapsed while the Earth cooled and became a solid planet which eventually developed its own climate and oceans with the simple forms of life (4,500-600 million years ago).

Saurischian
The major grouping of the dinosaurs (based on hip structure) in which the pubis is long and points forward, includes the sauropods (small coelurosaurs), and carnosaurs (big theropods).

Sauropodomorphs
Prosauropodomorphs and sauropods.

Sauropophlinne
A small crescent-shaped bone found at the tip of the lower jaw in ornithischian dinosaurs.

Sclerotic ossicles
Bony or horny plates found in the skin, particularly of reptiles.

Scutes
Bony or horny plates found in the skin, particularly of reptiles.

Sedimentary rocks
Rocks that have formed from sediments such as sands and clays.

Serrated
With a notched edge like a cutting edge of a saw.

Sinuses
Spaces within the body.

Slit
Of, or relating to the sun.

Solar species
From beneath (opposite of dorsal).

Species
A group of animals which look the same and can breed something which it is impossible to prove in fossil material.

Stratum
A rock layer.

Stromatolites
Banded rocks that were made by blue-green algae.

T

Terrestrial
One of the Earth's sympathy with the source of land-dwelling.

Tertiary Period
This follows the Cretaceous Period and charts the rise of mammals from 64 million years ago up to the recent past.

Tetrapods
Vertebrates with four limbs e.g. amphibians, reptiles, birds and mammals.

Theropods
A wide range of predatory dinosaurs, most of which were bipedal, including the coelurosaurs (small theropods), and carnosaurs (big theropods).

Tibia
The main shin bone (one of two, see also *fibula*).

Triassic Period
The first period of the Mesozoic Era, it lasted from 225-200 million years ago.

Tripodal
Of, or with, three feet.

Troodontid
The general condition or state (of a fossil specimen) in which muscles are attached.

U

Ulna
One of the two forearm bones (see also *radius*).

V

Variable gait
The ability to walk in a variety of ways depending upon how the legs are exposed downwards and forward from the hip socket.

Vascular
Of or relating to the blood.

Ventral
From beneath (opposite of dorsal).

Vertebrae
Animals with backbones, e.g. fish, amphibians, reptiles, birds and mammals.

Vertebra
Flat surfaces that are able to absorb the warmth of the Sun.

Z

Zygapophyses
Usually peg-like bones that help to hold vertebrae together, and prevent them from slipping apart.

INDEX

A
Albertosaurus, 14, 15
Allosaurus, 12, 13
Anapsids, 4
Anatosaurus, 30, 31
Anchiceratops, 38, 39
Ankylosaurus, 16, 17
Anhanguera, 13
Anthodemus, 13
Apatosaurs, 18, 19
Archosaurs, 4

B
Bactrosaurus, 30, 31
Bagaceratops, 35
Barapasaurus, 3, 5, 28, 29
Barosaurus, 22, 23
Bonaparte, Jose, 23
Brachiosaurus, 5, 20-21
Brontosaurus, 19

C
Camarasaurids, 5, 20-21
Camptosaurus, 30, 21
Carnosaurs, 5, 12-13
Centrosaurus, 5, 36-39
Ceratopsians, 5, 36-39
Cetiosaurus, 38, 39
Chasmosaurus, 38, 39
Coelophysis, 5, 6-7
Coelurosaurs, 5, 6-7
Compsognathus, 6, 7
Corythosaurus, 32, 33
Cynodonts, 4

D
Daspletosaurus, 14, 15
Deinonychus, 10, 11
Diapsids, 4
Dicraeosaurus, 19
Diplodocus, 5, 18-19
Diplodocids, 5, 18-19
Dromaeosaurids, 10-11
Dromaeosaurus, 8, 9
Dryosaurus, 26, 27

E
Edmontosaurus, 30, 31
Euoplocephalus, 46, 47
Euparkeria, 4

F
Fabrosaurids, 5, 24-25

G
Galton, Peter, 27
Gilmore, Charles, 21

H
Hadrosaurids, 5, 30-31

I
Ichthyosaurs, 4
Iguanodon, 3, 5, 28-29
Iguanodontids, 5, 28-29

J
Janensch, Werner, 21
Jensen, Jim, 21

K
Kentrosaurus, 42, 43
Kritosaurus, 31

L
Lambe, Lawrence, 33
Lambeosaurus, 36, 37
Leptoceratops, 5, 36-39
Lepidosaurs, 4

M
Mantell, Gideon Algernon, 29
Mantell, Mary Ann, 29
Megalosaurus, 17
Melanorosaurus, 32, 33
Muttaburrasaurus, 28, 29

N
Nemegtosaurus, 14, 15
Nodosaurids, 5, 44, 45
Nodosaurus, 44, 45

O
Omeisaurus, 23
Opisthocoelicaudia, 22, 23
Ornithischians, 4
Ornithomimids, 8, 9
Ornithopods, 4
Ornithosuchus, 4
Ouranosaurus, 28, 29
Oviraptor, 8, 9
Owen, Richard, 3

P
Pachycephalosaurus, 5, 40-41
Pachyrhinosaurus, 40, 41
Panoplosaurus, 38, 39
Parasaurolophus, 32, 33
Pelycosaurs, 4
Pinacosaurus, 46, 47
Plateosaurus, 5, 30-31
Plesiosaurs, 4

S
Saichania, 47
Ichthyosaurs, 4
Saltasaurus, 3, 5, 22, 23
Saurischians, 4
Sauropelta, 45
Sauropods, 5, 20-25
Saurolophus, 30, 31
Scelidosaurus, 5, 24-25
Shunosaurus, 31
Segnosaurs, 40, 41
Stegosaurus, 5, 42, 43
Struthiomimus, 36, 37
Styracosaurus, 31
Synapsids, 4

T
Tarbosaurus, 4, 15
Thecodontians, 4
Tenontosaurus, 24, 25
Thescelosaurus, 5, 26, 27
Torosaurus, 38, 39
Triceratops, 36, 37
Troodon, 8, 9
Tuojiangosaurus, 32, 33
Tyrannosaurids, 5, 14-15
Tyrannosaurus, 14, 15

U
Ultrasauros, 21

V
Velociraptor, 10, 11
Vulcanodon, 22, 23

Y
Yangchuanosaurus, 13